For We Know in Part

For We Know in Part

Two New Words For A Hungry Vocabulary

Stephen Morris

authorHOUSE®

AuthorHouse™
1663 Liberty Drive
Bloomington, IN 47403
www.authorhouse.com
Phone: 1-800-839-8640

Published by AuthorHouse   11/16/2012

ISBN: 978-1-4772-8357-8 (sc)
ISBN: 978-1-4772-8389-9 (e)

Library of Congress Control Number: 2012919893

CONTENTS

PREFACE

—◦•❋•◦—

"You know, I've never really thought about it like that" is the comment I'm looking for from my readers. Most other writers defending homosexuality focus on rebutting bad interpretation of the 'Clobber Passages', verses in the protestant Christian Bible used by fundamentalists to prove that heterosexuality is the only sexual orientation and that a homosexual is just a sick and depraved heterosexual.

First, let me say that this book does not follow the crowd talking about Bible verses mainly, although I do touch on them sporadically. I prefer to create metaphors and 'what-if' articles that prompt the reader to think more philosophically about ideas having to do with sexual orientation. Toward that end, I am introducing two words (heteronatural and homonatural) that immediately upon typing trigger the 'spelled wrong' wiggly red underline on my computer. Some day that will not happen because expanded use and acceptance will bring them into our daily vocabulary. I did not create them; one (homonatural) was actually copyrighted some time this year.

I did think of it on my own without any outside help in the morning minutes before I got up, but when I googled the word I found it was already in use. That's fine, but I wonder if it has ever been put to as much use as this book.

Sexuality is just one trait of our personalities along with a host of other aspects of what defines us. Since the words 'sex' or 'sexuality' stimulate such a negative and occasionally hostile reaction, why not use words that take the sting out of communication with words that signify much, much more than just one trait? So, throughout this book only the two new words are ever used unless I want to address sexuality more narrowly. It might cause you a little disconnect when you first encounter them, but I am certain you will learn to appreciate the substitution. (See chapter 3 for a wider discussion of this matter.)

Secondly, I want to thank my dear wife and gay son for their positive and helpful feedback on this project. I have turned our living room into a very messy writing studio that is beyond 'straightening up.' Doing so would cause me to lose the structure of my little piles. I also credit my wife with helping me to remember to tone down my language so she can understand it, thereby helping many others in the same way. "Thank you, dear. You're right."

Any names used in this publication are fictional to protect loved ones who are not in agreement with us from any embarrassment in facing their family members and friends who might direct unwanted and uninvited questions or comments to them. I am also using a pen name for that same reason.

INTRODUCTION

Besides myself, two other members of my family have approved of this book. Two other members would throw it in the trash (or hide it from their children) because it would offend them and their strictly literal understanding of the Bible. This book is what I want those two people to read someday, even if it's after I die (I'm 73 now). I'm also using a pen name so people who know me don't have to be feel embarrassed by that association.

For We Know In Part is primarily directed at heteronatural parents, family, and friends of gay and lesbian loved ones who have just come out of the closet. If you are one of these people caught in a scary place not knowing how to react, this book is for you. If your relationship with your gay loved one is more important than any other matter in your life, you will be comforted. If you are unsure about what to do or think or say, give this book a chance to help you answer that question.

For We Know In Part is a collection of essays that I originally wrote as handout brochures for persons interested in understanding homonaturality. Most of the articles are intended for supportive persons ministering to others who cannot quite let themselves approve of a sexual orientation other than heteronaturality. I have compiled these essays to expand on four 'fundamental' truths:

1. Sexuality consists of how one feels attracted to others (orientation) and how one responds to that attraction (behavior).

2. Traditional interpretation of Christian scripture does not consider homonatural orientation to be neutral like heteronaturality.

3. Because orientation has to do with knowledge that could not have been available to Bible writers, any interpretation of their writings that either denies homonatural orientation or condemns it is prejudicial. (Note: the root of the word 'prejudicial' is 'pre-judge.')

4. Because orientation has to do with knowledge that is still incomplete and possibly inaccurate, any Biblical interpretation by those of us supporting homonaturality that describes it with unswerving certainty is premature.

This book is like a quilt, each chapter being a stand-alone creation. The primary thread in this quilt is a thin, fragile, off-white strand of reason representing my belief that no one can ever know all there is to know about anything. No matter how long our tradition has supported the positions we take, we can never be absolutely certain we have heard the last word on the subject, neither from man nor God.

I need to be open to the possibility that my convictions are only as reliable as the latest revelation and that God can and does tell us more through people: prophets, scientists, and even our neighbors. That we only know in part, "through a glass darkly", is basic to how I understand truth. And, as I wait for a more perfect understanding, I will try to live a life of faith, hope and love, knowing that love is the most important of them all (please see the back cover).

I also need to approach most of those who disagree with me with an attitude of loving concern for them as faithful, well intentioned, Christians who feel very anxious about my threat to the sanctity of their Bibles. I need to acknowledge that they need the safety that rigid dogmatism provides without accusing them of hypocrisy or stupidity. Even though I cannot allow them to force their interpretation on me, I also do not want to ever be accused of trying to say to them, "This is what you must believe."

Note: Stephen Morris is a pen name. The subject matter of this book is still too sensitive for some people who are dear to me. I don't want them to be embarrassed or forced to discuss something they find so difficult to embrace.

CHAPTER 1

CHOOSING BETWEEN LOVE & TRADITION

When our son was a small boy, we might have agreed that everyone is heterosexual because there is only one sexual orientation and homosexuality is a perversion; or people can choose to be straight or gay; or because they embody evil, homosexuals can't be considered Christian. "Hate the sin but love the sinner" might have been something we would have said, but what it probably meant to us was "If you are gay, keep your distance and don't get close enough where we have to know you personally."

But as our son grew into a teenager and a young man, he so pleased his mother and me. With his faith, his honesty, creativity, sensitivity, and selflessness, . . . and his revelation that he was gay, how could we continue to feel the same way about homosexuality as we did previously? There was a strong clash between what we knew about our son's personality and character and what we thought we knew about homosexuality. Something had to give. We had to choose.

What we decided to do

If we had accepted traditional Biblical interpretation of homonaturality as being an abomination, unnatural, and sinful, we would also be forced to say that all the good and admirable traits of our son were phony. Was our closeness to our son less reliable than the traditional interpretation of Scripture? But then we noticed that our Bible also taught us: "A good tree cannot bear bad fruit." (Matt. 7:18) Because of what was plain to us about his character, we had to go with love and to be open to the possibility that we might be wrong about our understanding of Scripture on this matter.

Why we made this decision

Then it struck us that what is true for most people now might have also been true in ancient times. We believe that God did not choose to reveal to the ancients all that He reveals to us today or will reveal in the future. For example, didn't God let the ancients ascribe epilepsy to demon possession and accept slavery as a normal reality? It makes sense that 'sexual orientation' is also one of those mysteries that is only now being explained with any reasonable clarity. Because homonaturality as we know it today is a relatively recently defined orientation, it could not have been known to the writers of Scripture.

Yes, our understanding of sexuality has moved from superstition toward a point closer to science only in the last 120 years or so. The coinage of the word "homosexual" first happened in 1892 as a noun and in 1912 as an adjective, according to Barnhart's Dictionary of Etymology. The concept of a homosexual orientation obtained its first validation when the American Psychological Association in 1975 removed the term from its manual of mental disorders. What was once an oversimplified blanket condemnation of a whole group of people will, we believe, eventually be shown to be a complex but explainable phenomenon describing an un-chosen human condition that is as natural as heterosexuality.

History repeats itself

As we now look back with profound embarrassment at the way African slaves were treated by white people, so will all our descendants (black white, and in between) look back with similar regret at how homonaturals, most of whom just wanted to live with honor and integrity, were treated in our time. We have gone along with both injustices by not raising our voices in protest. We let our views of whole groups of people be dictated by the actions of an unrepresentative few. Stereotyping is wrong, especially when we condemn all homonaturals because of something we once saw in a movie or heard about from others. Would we let the world denounce all heteronaturals because of the few rapists among them?

Did tradition get it wrong?

The Bible writers, just like many of us, really could conceive of only one sexual orientation, heteronaturality. The perverse same-gender sexual activity they most frequently observed—fertility cult worship, pederasty (mentoring young boys for sexual favors), and public humiliation of conquered enemies—all bear out their understanding that such acts were unnatural for heteronatural people. Variations of orientation probably existed then, but there was no way that they could recognize them. All prohibitions against same-gender sexual conduct in both the Old and New Testaments of the Bible were written with the culture-bound assumption that God created Adam and Eve only, not Adam and Steve. But the fact is that God created humankind with variations of androgen and estrogen in every baby (Andrew & Esther?), producing a continuum of gender identities and orientations that are only now being properly understood.

Where are we headed?

Over the years we have come to know many other gay men and women, most of them possessing admirable traits and character, with the same imperfections and weaknesses as average people. They have similar moral struggles with the bad they don't want to be doing and the good they really want to do. We believe the majority of people of faith will eventually accept homonaturals as healthy and well-adjusted persons, hopefully by the time our grandchildren grow up. The enlightened church will then concede that being homonatural is a variation of sexuality, not a defect. At that point some legal accommodation will be extended to gay and lesbian couples honoring their enduring partnerships of love and devotion which mirror the lengthy marriages accomplished by heteronatural couples. It's just a matter of time. It always is. People do decide to be more loving once they see almost everyone else is. Then the church finds a way to do the same thing.

Well-meaning advocates of traditional Bible interpretation have suggested that homonaturality is a threat to family values. They say the Biblical model for marriage of one man and one woman is a moral absolute. When homonatural orientation is eventually proven to be a normal human condition, won't our acceptance of that fact, rather than destroying family values, actually help heal families split apart by the surprise revelation of a gay son or daughter? As to moral absolutes which might be at risk if traditional Bible interpretation is challenged, all I can say is this: **a moral absolute can not be defended faithfully if** it hurts people who do not deserve to be hurt.

Now that our son is a grown man we know from our study both in and in addition to the Bible that not everyone in the world is heteronatural. Many Christians, Jews, and Muslims and other persons not identified with any particular religious belief system are homonatural with integrity toward their sexual orientation. Our thought now is "Hate the condemnation, but love the condemn-or." To us that means "If you disapprove of homonaturals or people who support them, come a little closer. Once you get to know us, you'll be surprised at how natural we are." Then they too will face that conflict of what they know about us and what they thought they knew about homonaturality. And I guarantee they know less about homonaturality than they do about homosexuality.

Chapter 2

Rules & Principles: What's the Difference

When Christians are asked to be open to the idea of homonaturality, three big obstacles stand in their way: (1) the word 'homosexual' is loaded with negative meaning for them; (2) they can't accept any orientation other than heterosexuality; and (3) they can't accept the idea that people can be both homonatural and moral (or Christian) at the same time.

Let's do an experiment

First, let's talk about words. Say the word 'heterosexuality.' What comes to mind? It's hard to think of something, right? Maybe you have a faint remembrance of dating in high school, or the faces of special opposite-gender people in your life, but generally the word has no specific "jumps-out-at-you" meaning. I'm fairly certain your mind didn't think about rape, child molestation, or adultery, did it? And it's doubtful if any particular Bible verses came to mind either.

Now, say the word 'homosexuality.' What comes to mind? For most people, I'll bet, the most common picture that pops up is a cloudy but very negative impression of the most abnormal and indecent behavior one can imagine. It's different for everyone, but the H-word usually conjures up the last joke you heard on the subject, or a past time when you were offended by what you regarded as inappropriate behavior, or the impassioned instruction of your parents, pastor, or teacher that such activity is the most despicable conduct imaginable. For many people, certain Bible passages stand out as clearly rebuking what that word stands for, in their minds, that is.

We just can't seem to accept the H-word with the same neutrality we give to heteronaturality. Will the time ever come when both words are equally non-threatening? I believe they will, but not until the subject below is addressed openly and thoroughly.

Who would volunteer to be hated?

Second, let's talk about orientation. What about those people who claim that homosexuality is chosen by the person who claims to be gay or lesbian? There is some truth to what they say, but it is not what you would expect it to be. Before accepting their orientation, most homonaturals go through a phase where they resist the idea that they could be something other than heteronatural.

After all, who in their right mind would choose to be something so hated and looked down upon?

Who would want to go through life experiencing the judgment and ridicule, possibly being fired for no good reason, being evicted, being denied family employment benefits or hospital visitation rights, being forsaken by their families, exposing themselves to the danger of getting assaulted or murdered?

Yes, homonaturality does involve a choice

The choice for homonaturals is not the decision to BE gay, but a choice to stop resisting what they know to be true. In spite of all the reasons why it would not be wise to admit being homonatural, most gays and lesbians come to a point of personal integrity where they know they cannot deny who and what they are. A person can choose how to act out his/her orientation and can even choose to act contrary to his/her orientation, but the person cannot choose to discard that part of him/herself that is part of the fabric of his/her being.

Although the science trying to explain orientation is admittedly incomplete, there is a strong indication that homonatural people are the way they are because of something that happens to their physical and mental nature sometime after conception and within the first few years of life. It's probable that a condition is mapped out in the womb and then something hormonal during early childhood triggers the development of a homonatural nature before the child reaches an age where it can consciously choose what it wants to be.

People who are truly homonatural but act as heteronaturals are endangering themselves by going against their nature. I sincerely believe that science (and religion) will eventually help homonaturality to be understood by the vast majority of people to be a naturally different orientation, not an unnatural or defective one. At that point in time the mention of the word 'homonaturality' will conjure up the same degree of "so what?" that 'heteronaturality' does now. When 'orientation' reaches this level of acceptance, then how we define morality will change. Notice I didn't say "morality will change."

What I said was "how we define morality"; there's a big difference.

Rules and Principles: About Morality?

Lastly, lets do talk about morality. Part of this discussion must involve how we define morality. The RULES of morality (the do's and don'ts) of each generation change as time goes by, sometimes declaring something to be acceptable now which wasn't acceptable several years ago (bare ankles, make-up, jewelry, certain types of clothing, rock-n-roll music, dancing, or inter-racial marriage), to name a few). What don't change as much are the underlying PRINCIPLES that form the foundation of morality: honesty, kindness, compassion, selfless love, and faith.

Concerning morality within marriage, some rules have changed (polygamy, the father choosing a husband for the daughter, females having no rights), but the principles (devotion, protection, commitment) are more lasting. "One man/one woman" is just a rule that society might eventually decide is obsolete. The security of marriage or family is not dependent on people agreeing on what will undo it (rules). Rather marriage is tied to the conviction of what keeps it going (principles).

<u>CONCLUSION</u>

Wherever we can find a person of any gender who feels drawn to a single person of any gender with the same 'principles' of morality (selfless love, and faith, for example), marriage will survive the rule-change from one man/one woman to one person/one person. Wherever we can find a person of any gender dedicated to raising a child of any gender, the principles of parenthood (commitment and protectiveness) will outlast the rules of parenthood (one father/ one mother). Anybody who insists on making the rules just as important as the principles doesn't understand history or the lessons it has taught us.

So there you have it.

1. Words can be provocative or they can be neutral. It's up to us to decide how they affect us. Just as adultery, rape, and child molesting don't define what it means to be heteronatural, so also adultery, rape, and child molesting don't define what it means to be homonatural.

2. Homonatural orientation has already been recognized as a scientific reality. Someday what we understand about orientation will eventually be declared to be undeniable. When that happens, even the church, too, will once more adjust its doctrines to conform to popular practice or science already being accepted.

3. Principles out-live rules. Societies define rules, but principles have endured for eons. Rules change, but principles don't. Homonatural marriage and parenthood are threatening only to those who get these two ideas confused.

Chapter 3

A WORD TOO NARROW

Understanding the past

In the time and place that the book of Leviticus was written, human life and survival were very precarious. Certain assets were extremely hard to acquire and difficult to hold on to. Probably the most precious commodity to an ancient nomadic family and to the nation to which it belonged was not water, food, or livestock, but something far more fragile and less plentiful: the male substance that begets life, semen. The ancients believed that human sperm was limited and should not be wasted (Christian Science Magazine, Homosexuality and the Bible, by Walter Wink,(1996 p.2) With that understanding and with a high infant mortality rate from disease, war, pestilence, and superstition, the prospect of having and maintaining an enduring male family line was truly perilous.

The danger of losing some of its sons was so inevitable that the national mentality forbade upon penalty of death the wasting of male semen. Because of the extremely high value placed on the duty to sire sons, any social interaction by a male that permitted his semen to go anywhere but into a womb would have been tantamount to treason of the most dire kind. It is only natural that a strict prohibition (religious or otherwise) against same-gender sexual conduct would be enacted by such a people in order to minimize the loss of non-propagating semen.

While this compulsion to preserve the national identity was still in existence when the book of Romans was written, it was another influence of Greek and Roman sexual permissiveness that more infuriated the conservative Jewish mind. In the forms of religious cult temple prostitution by both male/female and male/male rituals, and of an institution called 'pederasty' (leaders mentoring young males for which sexual favors were expected), the society of N. T. times became too promiscuous for the Jewish and Christian faithful. It is no surprise that they would speak out against it in their writings. It was in this climate of perversion that persons born with or developing into a same-gender orientation would be pronouncing a death sentence upon themselves if they dared to declare their true natures.

In either the O. T. era of superstitious protectionism or in the N. T. era of reaction-ism, it was not safe for anyone to openly declare their same-gender love and affection. For some reason God had chosen to keep this reality obscure until a time in history when it would be less threatening for his people to announce their true identities.

<u>The problem with translations</u>

Bringing these ancient traditions and viewpoints to the mind of modern man has not been an easy task. Scholars have to choose modern words that sometimes only approximate the full meaning of the ancient words they represent. We know this to be so when you hear a Bible teacher expand his instruction by saying, "In the original Greek, this word had the additional connotation of . . ." Very often the translators have to make a human decision, an educated guess as to what word is best to use.

In some instances, translators do not just choose the best modern word to literally represent an ancient one. Sometimes they choose instead a word or phrase that best represents the prevailing theology of the subject they are deciphering. They make the translation say what they know their benefactors want to hear. In my opinion, this has most clearly happened with the interpretation of same-gender sexual activity. Because of a perceived aversion toward discussing sexual matters in general, translators have manipulated the ancient texts to also make them general and vague. The result is an misunderstanding of ancient texts by the laity that does not convey the individual significance of ancient Hebrew concerns and of the newer N. T. observations of same-gender sexual activity. We are then left to surmise that their understanding of those ideas is the same as ours. So we proceed to assign what we want to think as how they must have thought.

<u>A word too narrow</u>

Homosexual is a word we think we understand. It conjures up the most wicked behavior we can imagine and we never associate this word with decency or morality. It would take quite a stretch of our imagination to make that jump in reason. But what if centuries of misuse have programmed us to resist the idea that homonaturality could mean anything other than what we believe it to be?

My son is gay. He knows from Leviticus that the romantic feelings he has are reflective of behavior that book condemns. But in this country of over 314 million people he can't quite understand how his orientation is any threat to his nation's identity and preservation.

My son knows from Romans that it is a sin to use his sexuality purely for his own satisfaction, to exploit weakness in others, or to elevate his desires to the level of making them more important than God. He understands that these prohibitions are not obsolete and he tries to live his life controlling their impulse and minimizing their effect.

We have taught our son that it is not a sin to lift people up, to care for them when they hurt, to help end their loneliness, or to express affection for them in a committed romantic way. Gay people are capable of agape love too. They always have been, but they've never been as able as they are today to come out of the shadows to prove it. Society has always insisted on seeing people like my son, who is not perverse and idolatrous, as if he is. Is this just?

If the word 'unnatural' is intended to include those who don't misuse their sexuality along with those who do, it is a word far too wide. It is like the word 'cowardly' in Revelations 21:8 that states that cowardly people will be assigned to the "fiery lake of burning sulphur." In this text 'cowardly' probably refers to those people who choose to give up their faith because of the hardships of believing (ridicule, ostracism, persecution, torture, and execution). I'm sure you'll agree that the word 'cowardly' in this text never was meant to include those who suffer emotional panic due to psychological trauma (afraid of deep water, flying in an airplane, or standing in high places), or those who are reasonably afraid of disease, tornados, burglars, murderers, rapists, and terrorists.

To say that the word 'cowardly' in Revelations 21:8 refers to all people who are afraid in any circumstance would be the same as to say the words 'abomination' or 'unnatural' refers to every gay and lesbian. It is a gross misinterpretation of scripture. If the people of Bible times even had an understanding of homonaturality as we do today, Romans 1 would speak only to those gays and lesbians who used their orientation to abandon their faith and to profane the worship of their creator with idolatry.

We have two choices

Either we have to find another word to represent the sexuality of people like my son or we have to acknowledge that 'abomination' has a variety of meanings just like the word 'cowardly.' Maybe the newest ASV translation of 1 Cor. 6:9 says it best when it uses the phrase "homosexual offenders", which could imply that there exists homonaturals who are not offensive. The translators probably didn't intend to allow my interpretation, but real love would make that distinction.

Words are what we use to label ideas and actions. We do a terrible injustice to innocent people when we use general words to describe every specific situation. Real love would find a way to criticize a behavior it knows God does not like without attacking a behavior he very well might approve of. "homosexual" is a word far too narrow as it is being used today.

If you ever have a church hymnal in front of you, look up There's a Wideness in God's Mercy in the index and then look up the hymn. If the song has 5 verses printed, most likely verses 3 and 4 speak to the subject of this chapter. Many hymnals leave these veres out, probably because they consider them too radical.

CHAPTER 4

---·◦❋◦·---

WELCOME TO THE TABLE

(A belated invitation to estranged church-goers who happen to be homonatural)

You've been missed

The mainline churches have done you a great disservice. The very institution that should have been loving, compassionate, and understanding has failed for the most part to see you with the same welcoming spirit that they see each other. You are wrongly perceived by many as a threat to family values, doctrinal stability, and standards of decency. Your people have been cruelly treated without apology and often without proper explanation.

It would be very understandable if you don't want to have anything to do with the church anymore. If the way you've been treated is typical of faithfulness without love, why would anyone want to associate with that kind of hypocrisy? Your contempt for the prevailing religious attitudes would not be one bit surprising.

Having said that, I want to also state that not all of us feel the same as those who are shunning you, ridiculing you, threatening you, or abusing you. Some of us who are not gay have matured in our thinking to where we acknowledge your rightful place in society and the church of your choice. We want to see you have every benefit and blessing of religious affiliation that is available to everyone else. You've been deprived of a place at the Table for far too long. We want to say that you've been missed and we're asking that a place be reserved for you just in case you want to come back.

Whose table is it?

Please notice that I said a reserved place is being requested on your behalf. Who is being asked? Actually, I'm asking God to include you because it's His Table and I don't have a right to decide who can or can't sit there. The only requirement that I think He'd insist on is that those who come to the Table come attired in humility and openness, displaying a cooperative and encouraging posture toward others.

What does it mean to have a seat at the Table? It does not signify that you have a right to belong to any particular organization or to decide whom else can belong. It does not mean that you can control what is shared there? But it also does not mean that you have to conform to someone else's idea of perfection or acceptability. In fact, I doubt if the real Table would even fit within any human organization.

What's being served?

When the doctor examines a person complaining of illness, does she jump right to the diagnosis? No, she uses the process of elimination to rule out a variety of problems by thumping here, listening there, asking questions, and trying to set things in a time frame. It's a case of starting with the most basic possibilities and then working toward those more complex.

If we acknowledge that the most basic possibility for Christian responsibility is to love God fully (vertical) and to love our neighbor (horizontal) as ourselves (defining neighbor as those least like ourselves), then can't everything else flow out of that? We start with love and go from there. It's so simple; why do people want to make it so complicated?

The doctor's first rule is "Do no harm." Whatever doesn't fit within that motto is not pursued. The Christian's first rule is "If it isn't loving, don't pursue it." Yes, we can rationalize our criticism and judgmental-ism by calling it 'tough love,' but we have a second rule that says "Don't do what you wouldn't want to have done to you." A real commitment to these two rules should ideally steer us away from a misuse of love.

So, what's being served at the Table? The banquet theme is 'Assurance of Salvation.' The main entrée is 'love'. After that you can have your choice of a variety of side dishes: forgiveness, honor, respect, loyalty, compassion, friendship, encouragement, affirmation, inclusiveness, and a whole lot more. Different strokes for different folks, right?

What time does it start?

The Table is a kind of brunch buffet. You can come when you want and come as you are—no formal attire required, except you must have pants, shirt, and shoes (or contrition, willingness, and expectation). However, there is a time limit. Will there ever be a cut-off time? No one knows, but we're fairly certain that when that time comes, no allowances will be made for late arrivals. You know what they say about early birds? One more thing, when you arrive don't try to sit in the best seats; you'll find great admiration by starting out in the bleachers.

I'm sure that the host of God's Table doesn't even recognize denominations, doctrinal guidelines, or scholarly exegesis. All the attempts by humans to clarify what God intends or demands fail by comparison with the basic dual command "to love God" fully and "to love your neighbor as yourself." These statements don't require a lot of scrutiny to know what they mean. The example of the story of the Good Samaritan where an outcast is chosen to be the hero of the parable shows exactly how wide Jesus wanted the boundaries to be placed.

Do you need a ticket?

Yes. How do you get one? You must verbally acknowledge that Jesus is Lord in your life, that you're not able by yourself to live up to the laws God expects of His people, and that you're depending on God's promise that all who honestly say "Jesus sent me" will be admitted. Also you must invite someone else to come with you. Finally you must ask God's help to live in a way that exemplifies the trust you say you have put in Him. So, come on in! You're welcome at the Table, even if others don't think you are.

<u>Food for thought</u>

The fundamental obstacles for most people accepting homonaturality is the prevailing belief that the Bible condemns it. Because traditional interpretation of certain Bible texts erroneously asserts that homonaturality is synonymous with blatant promiscuity, condemnation is felt to be justified. People just seem unable to recognize that homonaturality is just like heteronaturality, that it is a separate and real sexual orientation that can be exercised in either a moral or immoral fashion. Both have elements that can be regarded as either good and bad, either natural and unnatural.

This faulty discernment can be combated in various ways, but I prefer to compare it with those feeble stances taken by persons (religious and political) of old who used their limited knowledge to inflict immense harm on innocent victims. The Inquisition and the Puritans, to name a couple, perverted religion by their intense persecution of believers who dared to think outside the box of conformity.

In our time leaders (religious and political) have put homonaturals under the curse of abomination, declaring all non-heteronaturals to be a threat to decency. Those people like Justice Scalia (U.S. Supreme Court, Lawrence v. Texas, June 26, 2003 dissenting), who feel marriage is threatened because the court decision invalidating sodomy laws in Texas are like the believers of old who balked at the declarations that (a) polygamy is contrary to God's desire for his children; (b) female newborns are not to be thrown away; (c) consent for marriage need not be sought by non-minors; (d) marriages performed by non-clergy are valid unions; or (e) inter-racial marriage is not immoral.

As the science of sexual orientation matures, the truth about the neutrality of homonaturality will emerge. At that time the pressure will be lifted from gays and lesbians allowing them to become worthy of respect in the minds of the majority of people, especially those who call themselves Christian. Then gay people will be judged just like everyone else, not by their sexual orientation, but by how they choose to live. No one can expect more than that.

CHAPTER 5

TWENTY QUESTIONS

The Problem

1. How many people believe that if we build an altar to the gods and goddesses of fertility and have public sexual intercourse in front of it, our crops will grow taller, our livestock will breed better, and we'll have more male heirs?

2. What if we bring captured soldiers to our country and then sexually humiliate them (making the males perform like females) in front of our citizens to show our power over our enemies?

3. What if we permitted the male leaders of our country to select young boys from our citizenry whom they will shelter, educate, mentor, and provide for their families for which these leaders may rightfully expect the young people to learn how to be sexually responsive to the desires of their benefactors?

4. Is it safe to say that we live in a different time and culture, and that regardless of what religion people of today embrace, only the smallest third-world minority would believe that such sexual activity as that described in nos. 1-3 has any positive effect on fertility, politics, or relationships?

5. Why, then, knowing that these social conditions were the pre-dominant contexts of which scripture writers in Bible times would have been aware of same-gender sexuality, do we insist on applying the words they wrote back then to persons today whose sexuality is in no way comparable?

6. How far out on a limb would you go personally, like a Berean, to find out just what the truth is?

The Solution

7. Do you know anyone who is either gay or lesbian who seems, apart from their sexuality, to be a good person?

8. If you do, have you ever discussed with them what their orientation means to them?

9. Are you acquainted with anyone who seems to be supportive of homonaturals?

10. Have you ever discussed with them why they feel that way?

11. Does it seem at all strange to you why so many good people are willing to go against traditional theology in their support of homonaturality?

12. Are you aware of any past circumstances where devout people flip-flopped from their opposition to something to supporting it and based both positions on their faith?

13. Do you have any idea of the exclusion, hate, and revulsion 1st century Jews had for gentiles?

14. Do you think it is significant that the hero of the 'Story of the Good Samaritan' was a gentile?

15. How hard a shift in faith do you think it was for early Jewish Christians to concede that gentiles were acceptable in God's eyes?

16. Do you think it's possible for God to create a human being with a mysterious and seemingly negative condition without explaining to the world why He still considers that person acceptable to Him?

17. If we don't condemn all heteronaturals for the failures of some of them, why do we reject all homonaturals that way?

A New Problem

18. Isn't what many of us think we understand about homonaturality today really just a blind subscription to misinformation from persons whose fear and ignorance over-power their reason?

19. How many of us declare that what we believe is just like what "Focus On the Family" teaches, or what the various denominational confessional statements declare, or what the pastor says we should believe?

The Final Question

20. Which would be worse: to have excluded a homonatural from fellowship and then find out later that we were mistaken in doing so, or to include him in fellowship and then find out we were wrong?

CHAPTER 6

---•❊•---

HAVE YOU EVER WANTED TO PET A SNAKE?

Ever wanted to rub the tummy of a giant boa constrictor?
Or cradle a python in your arms like a baby?

Fear often over-rides reason

Most of us react negatively to snakes. We don't need a reason; just keep them away from us. While some may have bad memories of an experience with a slithering creature, the majority of people in our culture are repulsed from snakes without ever having a personal encounter of any kind.

If the Bible was our only source of information about snakes or serpents, we might conclude that all snakes are bad. Snakes have no positive description in the Bible. The obviously most famous Biblical mention is that of the serpent tempting Eve in the Garden of Eden. Then there's the experience of the ancient Hebrews being bitten en masse in the wilderness after complaining of their suffering. Even though the subsequent "looking upon" the snake-like rod of Moses was designed for the healing of a snake's bite, the overwhelming message of the Bible is that snakes are dangerous, deceitful, and evil. Traditional fear and suspicion of snakes have surely been perpetuated in many people's minds due to Biblical influence.

Are snakes really evil? Of course not. How do we know? Education and experience have shown us good things about snakes: 1) any farmer will tell you that certain snakes control the over-population of various pests; 2) the venom of snakes is used to make serums to treat people bitten by snakes; 3) in some parts of the world, eating snakes is common; and 4) much study and documentation reveals that snakes are just another species of animal whose reputation is much worse than its real threat. No animal is inherently evil. Those with unpopular characteristics (snakes, sharks, alligators, etc.) can be understood and appreciated with a little study. God created every creature to be good; only man has decided otherwise.

Still we are divided in our confidence or desire to understand snakes. While some persons can distinguish between the danger and the naturalness of this species, many others cannot discard their revulsion no matter how much 'scientific' information is presented to them. It isn't that they necessarily hold only to the Biblical view of snakes, but their fear over-rides their intellect.

Salvation, not science

Why did scripture writers bequeath negative images of some animals? Two reasons: 1) they didn't know any better, and 2) their focus was narrowly purposeful. First, it is likely that their understanding of all animals was both limited and strongly influenced by superstition. Secondly, those writers were determined to pass on what they believed to be God's word for all mankind, not in expanding future generation's comprehension of biology. The image of the snake wasn't crucial to the dissemination of the truth of the image of God. Morality, faithfulness, separateness, and covenant were the core issues.

Ancient understanding of everything was primitive. God did not first reveal himself as the author of psychotherapy, electricity, moonwalks, heart transplants, or DNA. He was the creator of people and animals, of offspring, and of simple relational concepts. Man's God-given abilities taught him to distinguish between trust and fear, love and hate, fidelity and betrayal, loyalty and treason, and ultimately faith and doubt. But God revealed himself to his people at the level of understanding where they were—even though they may have been limited by superstition, culture, tradition, fear, and an extreme sense of self-preservation.

The Bible's message is salvation, not science. The Bible's 'science' conforms to the level of human understanding current at that time. Even though we now know, for example, that the body is formed by ovulation, fertilization, and cell-division, the writer of Psalm 139:15 was not wrong in regarding the formation of the human body as a mystery. He just wrote of what he knew (or thought he knew). The writer of Eccl. 11:5a might appear in error about the source and direction of wind in light of what we now understand about atmospheric pressure zones, but we understand his limited knowledge and don't regard him as either unintelligent or diabolical.

It's not important that a Bible-writer didn't understand the complexities of nature, science, or human development to teach us a lesson about morality and faithfulness.

But it is very important to know that a Bible-writer didn't understand the complexities of nature, science, or human development when we try to impose our modern understanding on those primitive writers.

I believe that God fully intends for mankind to eventually come closer to the real truth about many things that are described primitively in the Bible. I also believe that it saddens him that the church has traditionally been the last entity to affirm new discoveries. How many people have been wrongly ridiculed, tortured, or killed in the name of religion because they dared to challenge the church's understanding that

1. the earth is flat and has four corners;

2. the earth is the center of the universe;

3. the sun rises and sets;

4. persons that convulse are demon-possessed;

5. men and women must be separate in worship;

6. women must be silent in church;

7. the Bible supports slavery;

8. priests must interpret scripture for the laity;

9. the earth is less than 10,000 years old;

10. women who wear makeup or show their ankles are immoral;

11. men with long hair are immoral;

12. inter-racial marriage is immoral; or

13. the church cannot be challenged as to what is truth.

Reason usually has an uphill struggle

Homonaturality is a word that makes people just as uncomfortable as being in the presence of an un-caged snake. We know the very mentioning of the H-word, with or without accompanying explanation, will be received by many people in much the same way as if they were presented with a snake in a sturdy terrarium with a trained animal expert handling it. No matter how protected they actually are from the serpent's bite, some people's aversion to snakes transcends their brain's capability to accept that fact. The mere appearance of the image of a snake pushes a button in them. I believe their fear of snakes would not be diminished even if Jesus himself would hold their hands. Homonaturality can also be clearly explained so as not to be threatening, but the general reaction to that word is just like the unreasonable aversion many people have to snakes.

For people to come to a point of understanding about homonaturality (just like understanding snakes), they will need to make an effort to meet gay and lesbian people and 'handle' them gently and lovingly. People will need to question why homonaturals believe themselves not to be a threat to anyone. It won't be enough just to take someone else's word for it; it has to be a personal connection. By watching and listening to the real stories gay people have to tell, an inquiring mind might get to that point where reason over-rides fear instead of it being the other way around.

CHAPTER 7

---·❋·---

HOW TRADITIONALISTS VIEW HOMONATURALITY

On Feb. 22, 2003, my wife and I attended a conference entitled "Love Won Out." It was a 'Focus-On-the-Family' seminar in Austin, TX, organized with the declared purpose of "addressing, understanding, and . . . *preventing* homosexuality" (Conference Guide, Love Won Out, cover page.) Why did we go to such an event? Because we were asked by a friend from our church to listen to his side of this issue from a group he trusts at a one-day seminar for which he was willing to pay our registration of $80. We felt that if we honored his request, it would go a long way toward opening the doors of dialogue in our congregation that currently are not easy to open.

Now, did we learn anything positive from the conference? The answer is a definite, "Yes." By that I don't mean that they changed my mind about homonaturality, but I did learn more about how they think, about what parts of our position they consider most flawed, and about words and labels we may be guilty of using unlovingly.

First, the people I listened to believe that homonaturality is deviant behavior. To them It exists on the same level as pedophilia, bestiality, or pornographic addiction. They don't spend time talking about a homonatural person as being well adjusted and happy. I'm sure that many people who come to them with a story of confusion or struggle over sexual identity are viewed as persons who need to be rescued and changed, seldom encouraged to accept their 'orientation.' To them there is no such thing as a homonatural, only a sick and sinful heteronatural.

Second, they believe science must be resisted if it appears to contradict Scripture. I believe this is how they can stand opposed to all the major schools of thought in psychology and biology without feeling as if they're wrong. Science is bad science, in their minds, if it does not conform to Biblical truth, as they see it, of course.

Third, they see "Gay Agenda" behind our every plea for understanding. I'm sure we throw 'homophobic' around as much as they do 'gay agenda.' Maybe we're all a little paranoid about the danger the other side poses to us, but words are like bullets or arrows: once they're let go, they can't be controlled or called back.

Lastly, some of their literature does seem to encourage their churches to be less condemning and more loving. My skepticism forces me to ask if this is a sincere policy of concern or could it be a calculated ploy to play more appealingly to those who may have criticized their apparent fundamentalism in the past. It may be sincere, but with sort of a built-in caveat saying 'we aren't responsible if individual churches choose not to follow our advice.' I also believe they are trying to undo the negative effects caused by the label 'homophobic' without giving up their basic objections to homonaturality.

Hanging up our weapons

What did I tell my friend at church when he asked me what I got out of the conference? I conceded that it pleasantly surprised me to see literature encouraging their churches to be more loving and less judgmental. Why didn't I challenge their prejudice and his acceptance of it?

My goal as a defender of sexual orientation has always been to create conflict in the minds of those who disagree with me, to present them with an inconsistency between what they think they know about homonaturality and the attitude or character of people they oppose. If we can apply this principle of 'contra-distinction' to every potential confrontation or argument, I believe we can disarm our opponents with something they don't expect: an undeniably humble attitude and a non-hostile posture.

Someone said it something like this: a person can't be persuaded by reason if they have gotten to a place of intolerance without using reason to get there. Reason won't work on them. They expect us to argue. We should not give them what they are prepared for. Love, humility, and patience are the things they can't argue with. We have to find a way to listen to their viewpoints and acknowledge that some of what they tell us is beneficial to us and then let the Holy Spirit help them sort it out.

One more thing about Focus On the Family: they have applied the name *"Revisionists"* on those of us who seem to them to be 'revising' Scripture. While I deny that we're doing anything other than suggesting new ways to look at tradition just as the 'round-worlders' did or the 'carbon-daters' still do, I think the name is a good one if it means we're willing to accept change as a good thing. Obviously they can't.

A Parable

A flock of ostriches were wandering on the sandy plain when one of them thought he smelled a lion nearby. Screaming his alarm, all of them immediately put their heads in the ground (you know, to make themselves invisible to the lion if he should happen to come near). After a while, the first fearful ostrich's nose started to itch; he knew he would have to scratch it against his leg. Very carefully, he pulled his head out of the sand. As all of the other ostriches stayed locked in fear with their heads out of sight, the one ostrich looked around in amazement and exclaimed, "Hey, where'd everybody go?"

The fear of the lion's scent is the perception that homonaturality is to also be feared, opposed or eliminated. The ostriches with their heads in the sand are those persons who can't deal faithfully with that erroneous perception. The one whose head is out of the sand, but pretends he can't see any of the others is the person who uses his/her Bible to keep that error alive, avoiding the obvious truth that he/she can't afford to admit: if I concede that I can see the others, I'll have to admit that the practice of head-hiding doesn't work. It is easier to go along with the deception than it is to challenge tradition.

CHAPTER 8

---•❖•---

E.L.P.S.

Let's try to understand human relationships without all the negative labels, innuendo, and name-calling that seem to have taken over the sexuality scene today. Can we try to do a step-by-step analysis of how people relate to one another and decide in the process if what we've found is mutually acceptable or not? Obviously, we are on different sides of an issue, but we both quote the Bible and rely on the Holy Spirit to validate our certainty that we're right. It might seem like an insurmountable obstacle to come to agreement of any kind, but I personally believe it's worth the effort to try.

Where do we start? First we agree that both of us want to find common ground where our differences are not as important as our similarities. Second, we either drop all the jargon and find newer, less inflammatory words to describe the things on which we agree, OR we take the sting out of existing words so that they don't come out of our mouths with flaming darts attached. Third, we list the most basic types of relationships that human beings have and see what parts of them are acceptable to both sides.

<u>Step One: Acknowledging One Another</u>

Let me go first. There is no doubt in my mind that you are a person of faith, sincere in your outlook and committed to preserving the sanctity of the Bible. I think you believe that homonaturality is a depraved life-style and cannot by any stretch of the imagination be a God-favored activity. You honestly feel that marriage, family, and human values are at risk if homonaturality attains any degree of acceptance. I sense both your sadness and your indignation that anyone would ask you to change such deeply held beliefs, especially for a group of people whose behavior is so plainly sinful.

Now it's your turn. Let me try to write what I think you'd say if you were on the same page as me regarding step no. 1. Wouldn't you say "There is no doubt in my mind that you are a person of faith, sincere in your outlook and committed to . . . alleviating the pain and abuse of some homonatural people who consider themselves moral." That's probably about as far as you would want to go to acknowledge me, and that's okay for now. You're probably not at all convinced that I want to preserve the sanctity of the Bible or that I have any concern about the traditional definitions of marriage, family, and human values. Let's leave step one at this point and come back to these matters later.

Step Two: Neutralizing the Rhetoric

Can we agree that certain words connected with sexuality have lost their original meaning and been tossed into the manure pile? I'll concede that GAY is a bad choice for homonatural men. I want that word back like it used to be, don't you?: happy, gleeful, carefree? LESBIAN is okay, but I still mourn FAGGOT, DYKE, HOMO, and QUEER. Faggots, by the way, are bundles of kindling wood used to start fires. There once was the suggestion that it came from the time when fires were used to burn witches, or even that homonatural people were put in among the sticks, but my research doesn't bear that out. But it must have been perceived to be true by someone for the term to gain such wide use. I think some people think the story describes what they'd like to think really should happen to homonatural people.

I apologize for words like FUNDAMENTALISM and HOMOPHOBIC when they're used by people like me because they're usually loaded with negative emotion that's not always deserved by the persons we're trying to describe.

I'd like to take one more word off the table for now. That word is homosexual. The reason is this: I believe I can make a case for the fact that this word is too misunderstood to be a fair and reliable label for a whole group of people. You probably disagree at this point, but please just humor me for the moment and let us de-fang this word along with all the others mentioned so far. Since sexuality is just one aspect of a person's total personality, I thought it would be helpful to invent a word signifying more than just sexuality and that's why you have found this new word in my speech.

Step Three: How Do People Relate?

See if you agree with the following 23 statements:

1. People can relate to one another honestly or falsely. Right?

2. People can relate to one another morally or immorally.

3. People can relate to one another spiritually or secularly.

4. People can relate to one another romantically or with friendship.

Do we agree so far? Now let's change direction a little:

5. People can have good same-gender relationships.

6. People can show affection to persons of the same gender.

7. People can deeply love persons of the same gender.

We're wading up to our ankles, but we need to go in a little deeper:

8. People who relate to one another sexually should be responsible.

9. People who relate to one another sexually should feel a life-long commitment to the well-being of the other person.

10. People who relate to one another sexually without a life-long commitment to the well-being of the other person are behaving immorally from a Christian standpoint.

11. Heteronatural people are capable of statements 1 through 10.

Now you have to make a little jump (maybe a leap) in reason to follow me with the statements that follow:

12. People who are physically attracted to persons of their same gender are also capable of statements 1 through 10.

Here is where I lost you, right? How could I possibly make a statement like that and expect you to agree with it? Okay, 'let's start over' and keep it basic:

13. All people have two sides to their sexuality: (1) what their minds tell them about their sexual desires (orientation) and (2) how their minds tell their bodies to respond to that information (behavior).

14. All people are responsible for how they respond (behavior) to what their minds tell them, but they can not control the way their minds work (orientation).

15. Heteronatural people are described by statements 12 and 13.

Now for the finale:

16. Heteronatural is a word that describes both the good and the bad a person can be as he/she relates to persons of the opposite gender. It involves both orientation and behavior.

17. As it stands today, the H-word only applies to behavior. It is not recognized by most heteronaturals as a label for orientation because they believe there is only one sexual orientation.

18. If sexual attraction (orientation) to persons of one's own gender is someday proven to be a scientific reality, a word will have to be used to identify that fact. It can't be the old H-word if that label is reserved for behavior only, OR it can be the old H-word if it is given the neutral connotation that 'heteronatural' enjoys.

Okay, it's fine with me if you think 1-11 and 13-17 are the only statements you can agree with. That's understandable, but I want to go on the record right now to tell you that nos. 12 and 18 are being worked on by faithful people who really believe the time is coming when these ideas will be included in the ELPS: Eternal List of Paradigm Shifts. What's a 'paradigm shift.'

It's a major re-thinking of something that once would have been unthinkable. This list includes statements like:

19. The world is round.

20. The earth is not the center of the universe.

21. Gentiles have a place at the table.

22. Males don't rule the planet.

23. Slavery is immoral.

What is the church's record concerning nos. 19-23? Nothing to brag about, right? I think you're going to find that sexual orientation is one more 'truth' that the church is going to have to eventually accept.

CHAPTER 9

·❈·

WHAT IF YOU HAD LIVED BACK THEN?

(Note: while I said previously that this book was primarily directed to persons whose loved ones may have just revealed they were gay, this particular chapter is more aptly aimed at persons who can't give up their biblical opposition to homosexuality so easily.)

If you could have lived in the 11th century in a social and spiritual environment similar to the one you now enjoy, you probably could have been one of a variety of people: maybe (1) an illiterate peasant, (2) a more enlightened aristocrat, (3) a well-learned religious leader, or (4) an independently-thinking merchant. Regardless of your intellectual identity, your life would have been strongly influenced by the strangler-hold the Catholic church held over governments and secular institutions. Because your church had already investigated matters of spiritual importance, you probably would believe, like the majority of Christians in your day, what the church fathers told you to believe. That conviction would be based on a long tradition and your certainty that the church leadership could be trusted to define what 'truth' is.

At such a time as that, you would have been witness to what the church did to persons who dared to question time-honored doctrines and papal pronouncements. You would have seen public ridicule and harassment. You might have heard about people who were tortured or executed by hanging, burning-at-the-stake, or drowning. You would have heard the official disapproval of Jews, Muslims, and heretics of all kinds. And you would have lived under the continual threat of excommunication, quite possibly the most potent weapon the church held over its people.

But you also might have marveled at how a few ordinary people stubbornly refused to recant their alleged error and were willing to face death rather than to repent and avoid punishment. You might have had neighbors who risked their lives and the lives of their families by declaring that they believed the 'new sciences' about the earth being round instead of flat, about the earth, not the sun, being a planet in motion, and about the probability that our galaxy was not the only planetary system in the universe.

Putting yourself in their shoes, what could you possibly say to the guardians of scripture and tradition in the 11th century if you really felt there was some merit in the idea that the world was not flat? What would you say to prove to them that they were wrong?

You would not have known then what you know now

Back then those who knew scripture would have assured you that the Bible accurately defends every official doctrine of the church. It would have been very threatening for you to question the 'official' position. And you wouldn't even have wanted to question it; you would have been perfectly content to go with the flow and even defend the sanctity of traditional interpretation. After all, being out of step with the church's position meant certain disapproval, ostracism, economic hardship, and (worst of all) pronouncement of excommunication. Who in his right mind would go out on that limb? But for you it wouldn't be a matter of risk because you would be contentedly secure in the knowledge that those advocates of the new science were fanatics, too corrupt and misinformed to be given any credibility whatever.

Do you think it would be possible to live in that time and really recognize that the sum of man's knowledge in the 11th century is not as complete and reliable as it would be in the future, say, for example, in the 21st century? Could you really have visualized how much difference 1000 years could make about what you thought you knew and believed? Probably not. Because you couldn't have known then what you know now, you would not be in a position to acknowledge that you (or the church's learned scholars) were extremely deficient in what you think you know.

What would have it taken for you to be questioning?

Most likely, unless you, personally, were close to someone accused of heresy, someone respected and trusted who was known to be a faithful, reliable, down-to-earth, decent person, you would not feel a need to question what equally faithful reliable, down-to-earth, decent people were teaching. Not until you experienced the loss or threatened loss of someone you love would you even be faced with the decision whether or not to investigate the matter.

However, if you weren't illiterate and had some exposure to knowledge of that day, you might possibly have been a person who believed in giving new ideas a little attention just as long as they didn't force you to choose between traditional wisdom and unproved speculation. You probably could have walked a little way down the 'road of controlled curiosity' just because you considered yourself a little more enlightened than the general population.

But how much further would you walk if you had been a scholar with access to information not generally available to the common person? Might you have been a person who could have remembered or have learned how some older ideas from your heritage were no longer considered reliable in light of 'modern' realities, modern for the 11th century, that is? Even though the modern ideas of the 11th century were not yet fully explained, you might have become persuaded that they made more sense than those which you had been swallowing for as long as you can remember.

Now come back to the present

It comes down to this. Was tradition and incorrect interpretation of the Bible so strong that the people of the Dark Ages could not break free of the ignorance and fear that held them in doctrinal bondage for so long? Obviously not, because we don't believe like they did, do we? But it took a long time and many innocent people had to suffer and die for believing in ideas that were diametrically opposed to official teachings.

Now the larger problem is this: "Are we so arrogant as to think that our tradition is above questioning?" Will we make the same mistakes they did and refuse to examine ideas that may seem just as foreign to our ears as the notion that the world is round must have sounded to their's? How long will it take and how many more innocent lives will be ruined or lost before the church of today admits they can't know as much as people will know 1000 years from now?

CHAPTER 10

ANCIENT UNDERSTANDING OF SLAVERY &
DIVORCE

Is there any relationship between opposing something the early church tolerated and accepting something the early church condemned?

Does the Bible really condemn homonaturality?

Slavery coexisted with the early Christian church and also with the O.T. Hebrew theocracy. Persons could be brought into physical bondage by various means: (1) selling themselves into servitude, (2) being kidnapped and sold, or (3) being enslaved as a consequence of military defeat. Whatever the reasons for the slavery we encounter in the Bible, we have no example where any Bible writer ever told readers that slavery is perverse, immoral, or illegal. Back then people of faith didn't think it important to make an issue out of something that we find so repulsive today.

Ask yourself, 'If any person today would appear for church membership seriously declaring himself to be the owner of slaves and that he had the right to do anything he wanted with his own slaves, would he be welcomed in our church? Or would that church, if it accepted him, be welcome within any of our denominations' conferences? If that person told us that what goes on between himself and his slaves in his household and especially in his bedroom is nobody's business but his own, would we turn a blind eye and pretend that it doesn't matter? If a person had no slaves, but declared that he believes in the right to own slaves and do with them as he sees fit, would we draw the line and shout "Not here, you don't."

One might argue that comparing slavery to homonaturality is not valid just because slavery was allowed to change as society changed; it was not a matter in which the church involved itself. That same person might argue that we cannot change what the church took a stand against. If that is so, what do we do with divorce?

Jesus condemns divorce

Jesus clearly instructed his disciples in Mark that divorce on any grounds is wrong and in Luke that divorce on grounds other than unfaithfulness was immoral. If we interpret this teaching literally and press for its application today as strongly as it was pushed in the early church, many church members would find themselves living as "practicing sinners" and eventual targets of expulsion. There would be no gray area of interpretation.

SORTING IT OUT

But scholars 'read into' Jesus' instruction the reasoning behind his statement. They explain that Jesus was probably aggravated with the ease with which men of his day could divorce women and thrust them indefensibly into a situation of poverty, ridicule, and vulnerability. His intention, they rationalize, was not to prevent divorce on any grounds other than unfaithfulness, but to protect womanhood from conditions that the society of their day was not ready to address. It was a matter of opposing one narrow thing to prevent the wider disaster of another thing. The argument evolves that in our day and age, protections have been put in place to protect women who get divorced and therefore literal application of Jesus' command to modern society is unnecessary.

Homonaturality is comparable

It is just this leniency that proponents of 'sexual orientation' and responsible sexuality wish to propose to their critics. Just as the wider modern application of divorce laws can fit comfortably within the apparently narrow prohibition of Jesus' day, so also the wider understanding of moral same-gender attraction can fit within the equally narrow prohibition of man-lying which Bible writers condemn. In both cases—divorce and sexuality—ancient understanding and practice could not anticipate the development of the modern expression of our responsible and moral fellow Christians.

Bible interpretation often conforms to popular practice

The problem for the early church was not that all man-lying was wrong; the problem was that their society saw man-lying only as an expression of idolatry or lust. It was not against just the idolatry of "making something more important than God" we experience today, but rather the perverse orgiastic reenactment of seeds-being-planted and animals-being-impregnated that Israel's idolatrous neighbors practiced. It was a case of opposing one narrow thing to prevent the wider disaster of another thing.

So, in both cases, divorce and sexuality, something good and permissible was over-shadowed by the fear of something truly terrible and disgusting. All we have to do is to let our minds accept the fact that 'time' always offers new societies a way to change and still be faithful to the laws they hold sacred. Those laws aren't always literally imitated in successive societies, but the principles behind them do perpetuate their foundation.

The principles are: *GOD IS LOVE.* **GOD SEES GOOD THAT MEN CAN'T VISUALIZE. GOD DOESN'T SEE EVIL WHERE MEN INSIST ON PLACING IT.** GOD'S LOVE IS IN ACTIONS, NOT ONLY IN WORDS, ESPECIALLY NOT PRINTED WORDS. We have to overcome our tendency to want to take of the forbidden tree and eat. It isn't that we'll know what God knows; it's that we'll think we do.

CHAPTER 11

STEREOTYPING BY THE CHURCH?

Almost all of us are 'gentiles'

Almost every person who attends a Christian church today anywhere in the world must identify with a word from the early Christian church. That word is 'Gentile.' Without the events of Acts 10 and Paul's ministry, persons outside the Jewish faith would not have been welcomed into the church of Jesus Christ in the numbers it enjoys today. If Peter had not had his vision and if Paul had not had his 'road-to-Damascus' experience, quite likely we would not have the multitude of non-Jewish denominations we have. We would still have denominations because language and geography will always have a way of separating people apart, but those denominations would most probably be Jewish in nature and practice.

Think about the effort it took to accept gentiles

How dramatic was it, do you think, for the early Christian church to open its doors to Gentiles? What was Peter's response to the voice telling him to kill and eat food that the typical Jew is forbidden to eat? This new instruction was gigantic, humongous, un-heard of. In fact, it caused a great disturbance in the church before the issue was finally settled. If it had not been resolved, you and I would probably not have been reading this book together.

Imagine what it might have meant to a 1st-century Gentile to be invited into a community of faith once reserved for only Jews. Wouldn't he surely ask at some point, "If I'm acceptable to you now, what about my grandfather and grandmother? Where are they included in God's plan for humanity? Why wasn't it communicated to them that they too were acceptable?" In other words, how is it that persons once regarded as "dogs" (Mk. 7:27) even by Jesus are somehow made acceptable to enter the family of faith? Today we would call it a 'paradigm shift,' wouldn't we? How did we define 'paradigm shift' earlier? It's a major re-thinking of something that once would have been unthinkable.

Did Paul ever perpetuate a stereotype?

Even Paul whose ministry was devoted mostly to the conversion of gentiles could not free himself from a language that allowed him to have a condemnatory attitude toward some of them. In Eph. 4:17ff he reveals this wording limitation: " . . . *you must no longer live as the Gentiles do, . . . 18They are darkened in their understanding and separated from the life of God because of the ignorance that is in them due to the hardening of their hearts. 19Having lost all sensitivity, they have given themselves over to sensuality so as to indulge in every kind of impurity, with a continual lust for more."*

Obviously he doesn't mean 'all' gentiles because he's writing to some of them who have committed their lives to Christ. Either Paul didn't know of another word to distinguish a gentile convert from a gentile pagan OR he just felt his readers would know what he meant. But the word 'gentile' in his time had taken on such a negative and offensive meaning that its use could be potentially hurtful if thoughtlessly applied to all people without considering which among them might be innocent of the label.

CONCLUSION

The same kind of 'insensitive generalization' is built into the word 'homonatural' today. The very mention of the label brings total depravity to the mind of many without considering which among that group might be innocent of the label. Are all homonaturals idolatrous (Rom. 1), lustful, promiscuous, or perverse? Or is it time for a re-thinking of what once was considered unthinkable?

Now that I have encountered homonatural people who are definitely not idolatrous, lustful, promiscuous, or perverse, I have to conclude that not all homonaturals deserve to be included in the umbrella of ridicule that stereotypical attitudes perpetuate. I also urge those of you who have not met such normal and natural people to stop pushing them away from you so that you, too, can come to the place where your fear doesn't over-ride your reason.

CHAPTER 12

WAS FILTHINESS EVER NEXT TO GODLINESS?

This chapter is based on numerous facts taken from Chapter XIII (Miracles to Medicine) of A History of The Warfare Between Science and Theology in Christendom (1896) by Andrew Dixon White (co-founder of Cornell University). The entire work is in public domain at http://abob.libs.uga.edu/bobk/whitewtc.html. It is a very informative and eye-opening look at past 'heroes' of religion who were in many ways primitively backward in their world views.

Use your imagination

Picture a scene where everyone is walking around dirty and smelly. No one ever takes a bath, washes their hands, or changes their clothes. You cannot use the word unhygienic because this sight is taking place at a time in history when society had no word for hygiene. Human waste was dumped in the streets. The public water supply was a nearby stream or pond, which was not protected from contamination. No one had any concept of bacteria, germs or susceptibility to disease. Now try to imagine that if anyone does try to bathe or wash in any way, then family, neighbors, and the church especially, which dictates the requirements of such living, will cruelly look down on such a person as vain or prideful.

This situation existed because, first of all, church leaders once believed that because mankind was created in the image of God, it was, therefore, considered sacrilegious to tamper with the natural state of a divine creation. Also, making oneself clean was a sign of pride and vanity that was forbidden in scripture. The populace, dependent upon the educated clergy for instruction and guidance, had no way of being aware that they were being misled by pious, but biased, minds.

Every waking moment was devoted to appeasing those malevolent divine forces that constantly caused storms, floods, earthquakes, fires, injuries, and diseases. Failure to control one's behavior would result in the birth of handicapped children. Prior to Benjamin Franklin's lightning rod experiments, the church assigned lightning in storms to an evil power. The church also believed that the ringing of bells during violent storms would somehow disperse the storms by agitating the air.

Where the church once stood

As the church sanctioned miraculous relics and superstitious healing, evolution of the medical arts was held back hundreds of years. Tertullian, St. Gregory of Tours, and St. Ambrose taught the sinfulness of appealing to medical treatment over the application of divine interventions such as prayer and the laying on of hands. Enormous income was realized by church institutions which claimed to possess certain holy objects: bodies, body parts, as well as possessions of saints and other famous relics which could give the buyer deliverance from divine wrath. Because superstition created such vast revenues, why would any institution favor development of the knowledge that would undo its source of income?

The church was the chief opponent of surgery and anatomical studies because such practices violated the temple of the Holy Spirit. The Apostles' Creed with its emphasis on resurrection helped foster the conviction that mutilation of the body might somehow interfere with going to heaven. Various papal decrees between the 6th and 13th centuries forbade study of medicine and surgery (quoting O.T. scripture where King Asa trusted in physicians and died). Physicians were classified until the 15th C. with sorcerers and magic-mongers. ("Where there are 3 physicians, there are 2 atheists." Bull of Pious V). Thomas Acquinas believed the forces of the body were independent from its physical organization and should be studied through philosophy and theology rather than through anatomical study.

Among the ideas strangely accepted even by intellectuals in the middle ages were these: the brain increases or decreases its activity with phases of the moon; humor in people increases or decreases with tides of oceans; the lungs fan the heart; the liver is the seat of love; and the spleen is the seat of wit. Since it was believed sickness was God's punishment for sin, it was considered sinful to interfere (inoculation, vaccination, anesthesia, surgery) with divine purpose. Resistance to anesthesia, for example, was not effectively overcome until the 18th C. when a Scottish doctor named Simpson quoted Gen 2:21 to show he was merely imitating God's action of putting Adam to sleep.

What does this mean for us?

All through time religious leaders have used scripture and the power of their office to control the progress of human thought and, in most cases, to hold it back from its full potential. Discoveries, breakthroughs, and inventions were delayed because church leaders held control over a populace that danced to its manipulations. Name the discipline and the church has slowed its development with well-meant, but obviously destructive, ignorance and held back its growth with superstition: anthropology, astronomy, biology, chemistry, medicine, meteorology, physics, or psychology. Even in recent times, the church has often been the last institution to accept ideas and science that the rest of the world already acknowledges.

Sexual Orientation, although not yet fully understood by the scientific community, is evolving as a congenital/pre-pubescent reality that will eventually be accepted as a distinctively separate human condition that distinguishes heteronaturality from several other orientations. You can be sure many lives will have been ruined or destroyed in the time that it takes the most conservative theologies to accept this new truth.

We need to open our minds and hearts to do what Jesus would do. Jesus would understand the difference between natural predisposition and perverse choices. He would hold all orientations to the same standard: "love your neighbor as yourself." He would permit each age to define its concept of marriage in such a way that fosters devotion and commitment and avoids selfishness and exploitation even between persons of the same gender. I do not know if God will ultimately forgive those of us who resist this advancing of human understanding, but he will surely be disappointed in us for taking so long to do so.

CHAPTER 13

·❈·

THE ONLY GOOD INDIAN IS A DEAD INDIAN*

The author apologizes to Native Americans for using this title, but it is hoped that the reader will sense the prejudice and hatred against 'Indians' (derogatory term) in the old west as being comparable to that directed against the minority group that is the subject of this article.

Making a comparison

When the government of the United States established treaties with the American Indians during the 19th century, the integrity of the persons entering into the agreements as "representatives of the U.S." was not always certain. But for the illustration of a basic truth I want to teach, let us borrow the idea of 'treaties' in our discussion of the question "Who represents the truth about homonaturality?"

The average citizen of the 'old West' didn't accept the validity of a treaty because a general sat down with an Indian chief and they made promises to each other. That event was not even appreciated by the vast majority of citizens except on a newspaper page that appeared a month later or by word of mouth. For these people, the 'truth' about peace is what they experienced, not what they were told took place a thousand miles away.

The authority of a peace agreement was tested by the encounters of citizens from each side on the prairie, along the riverbank, or near small settlements. As we have learned from our history books, these encounters were often not honorable toward native Americans. So, whenever one would speak of treaties in the Indian camps or the frontier towns, it was natural that the image which would come to mind would have been one of how the treaty was broken, who offended who, and what burden was left for the survivors to bear for the rest of their lives. The misconduct of the offenders was often so gross that those persons who considered it afterwards attributed the acts of the perpetrators as being typical of all Indians, most of whom just wanted to live quietly and peacefully with everyone. That's how the unfortunate expression was born which claimed "the only good Indian is a dead Indian."

'All' are not the same as 'some'

Just as the marauding Indian was not a true reflection of all Indians, I believe that homonaturality is being broadly judged because of the actions of a narrow minority. Just as most people were not interested in getting to know Indians as individuals, so also heteronatural minds cannot even contemplate what it would be like to get acquainted with homonatural people and to know them personally.

Think of the prejudice built into the word 'Indian.' It ignores the fact that native Americans come from a multitude of varying tribes. It presumes that every member of every tribe has no individuality, no worthily unique out-look or opinion, and no distinctive heritage. It just labels all people with a generalized perception that is negative. Even if some people don't attach negativity to their use of the word 'Indian,' it still reflects a desire not to get to know them very well and a willingness to buy into the inaccurate stereotypes most people have concerning them.

The same generalized prejudice exists toward people who are non-heteronatural. In the minds of most people, the word 'homonatural' conjures up the most depraved images of sexual behavior, much like the word 'Indian' would have frightened people in the old west to run for cover.

Interpreting scripture through clouded glasses

'Homosexual' does not accurately describe the people mentioned in the Bible. Those are the persons who broke the 'treaties' of morality, of decency, and of faithfulness that God made with his people. Their misconduct was so gross that the persons who considered it afterwards attributed the acts of the perpetrators as being typical of the masses who just wanted to live quietly and peacefully with everyone. That's why the judgment against homosexuality has reached the unjust extreme where many people feel that homosexuals deserve to be killed.

It might appear that God has seen fit to not publicize His 'treaty' with homonaturals, but this is not the case. They are included in the command to "love your neighbor as yourself." The very example of this instruction by Jesus was a story of two persons encountering one another, one a Samaritan and the other a Jew who were as companionable as a homonatural and a fundamentalist (or an Indian and a pioneer). Do you remember which one was described by Jesus as the hero of the story? Why do we insist on reversing the characters when we apply that story to our walks of faith? It was not the traditionalist who gave aid; it was the outcast, the despised one. Think about it!

Anyone who reads Romans 1 with honesty cannot fail to see the connection between the behavior described there and the sin of idolatry. Identification of to whom the pronoun "they" in verses 21 to 32 refers is crucial to a proper understanding of this text's perceived railings against homonaturality. "They" are the ones defined in verse 18: *men who suppress the truth by their wickedness.* It does not refer to every person who is gay.

<u>Getting it 'straight'</u>

The writer of Romans 1 was generalizing when he spoke of the depraved condition of gentiles which developed after God's natural wholesome indwelling was resisted and thrown aside by them. Choosing to engage in self-deception (v. 21), their conduct evolved downward to the vilest and most detestable forms of expression. Generalization is evident in Romans 2:1 where the author gathers in the reader (Jews, in that time) as being guilty of the same offenses. So the indictment fits all people as is similarly recorded in Rom. 3:23 and Psalm 14 (& 53). Included in that spiraling degeneration under the label "malice" in Rom. 1:29 are those misguided individuals who erroneously single out verses of scripture to condemn groups or OTHER individuals for things they don't understand.

Look how long it has been since the last Indian tribes were 'pacified.'** What is their condition now? Where is our respect for such a wide variety of cultures that existed self-sufficiently before our 'enlightened' ancestors came to these shores? What did our white forefathers bring with them? They brought superstition, fear, ignorance, prejudice, and disease. They showed the tribes how to hate and abuse. Guess what; we're still doing that to one another, although now we have found another group to despise.

***<u>A final apology to Native Americans</u>: this author has no desire to exploit trauma in your heritage. Whatever your circumstances may be today, they could have been a whole lot better if my ancestors had acted more honestly, responsibly, more honorably, and more sensitively toward your ancestors.*

Chapter 14

WHAT DO HOMONATURALS REALLY WANT?

Homonaturals want the world to understand that:

1. <u>Though they can't explain it, they did not choose to be homonatural.</u> There is choice involved in deciding to acknowledge what your body is telling you: that you find persons of your own gender more attractive than the opposite gender; that your romantic dreams are about your own gender; and that you're very unhappy trying to be heteronatural.

2. <u>Homonaturals are just like heteronaturals in every way,</u> some good and some bad, some responsible or some irresponsible, some moral and some immoral, honest and dishonest, industrious and lazy, selfless and selfish, prone to loyalty and prone to betrayal, some holding sexuality on a high plane and some being totally depraved, some very devout in the Christian faith and some having no interest in religion, some God-favored and some probably not so favored.

3. <u>Homonaturals are just as capable of long-lasting monogamous relation-ships as heteronatural people.</u> You can't go by numbers unless you concede the percentages. If homonaturals make up a certain percentage of the general population, don't look for the same number of durable unions as heteronaturals. And don't look for the same percentage of durable relationships in a group that has no comparable legal standing to heteronatural marriages. Just admit that not all gay and lesbians are promiscuous sex addicts. In fact, please concede that not even the majority is of such persuasion.

4. <u>Homonaturals can live up or down to the expectation you have of them.</u> The gay community is made of individuals, some of whom just like heteronaturals are 'givers' and 'takers.' If you're looking for 'takers,' you'll find them in either orientation. If you're open to finding 'givers', they're there also. If you know how to distinguish the two, you won't be disappointed.

5. <u>The actions of the minority are not characteristic of the majority.</u> The two rules-of-thumb in bigotry are to believe (1) that what is true of one is true of all, or

(2) that those who belong to the group must bear the stigma of the few whose actions are despised.

6. <u>No one is in danger for being in the vicinity of a homonatural</u> unless they put themselves in jeopardy by being irresponsible. The danger is the same no matter whether someone intent on hurting them is homonatural or heteronatural.

CHAPTER 15

—◦◦◦—

WHAT DO SAY TO MISINFORMATION BY CRITICS

As persons who do not approve of Homonaturality communicate with those who do, inevitably the conversation eventually includes sentences like "We're all sinners" or "we love the sinner, but hate the sin." I have gathered those two insults here along with nine more that are very common.

1. <u>We're all sinners.</u>

This statement immediately implies that just being homonatural is a sin. It reflects a mindset that all homonaturals put themselves against the Bible and traditional Christian doctrine. Then the speaker seems to extend an olive branch by conceding that sinner-hood applies to everyone when, in fact, the speaker most likely doesn't really believe that his sin is as bad as that of homonaturals. A homonatural Christian also believes himself to be a sinner, but in the same way as a heteronatural; naturally inclined to selfish conduct, unable to restore himself to God's favor, and relying on the sacrificial mercy of Jesus to redeem him.

2. <u>The Bible plainly teaches that homonaturality is a sin.</u>

The Bible plainly teaches that unnatural, idolatrous (Romans 1), and self-serving sexuality is a sin. It is modern translators that have applied the word 'homosexuality' to that type of behavior. It would be the same as saying that 'heterosexuality' is a sin because of adultery, rape, pedophilia, or the shrine prostitution so prevalent in ancient times.

3. <u>Love the sinner, but hate the sin.</u>

Again, to equate homonaturality with sin is to judge some people whose behavior isn't perverse, or even sexual, along with those the speaker of that phrase finds so contemptible. It pre-judges a whole group of people based on the erroneous perception that homonaturality is not a neutral orientation like heteronaturality.

4. The Bible doesn't recognize sexual orientation.

The Bible writers didn't know about sexual orientation. It comes under the same category of modern understanding as psychology, neurology, astronomy, avionics, transplantation, and thousands of other scientific discoveries.

5. Threat to marriage and family values.

Homonaturals agree that perversion is a threat to marriage and family values, but they do not agree that being true to one's orientation in a responsible way is the same thing. Until people can see gays and lesbians as individuals, they will continue to make the biggest mistake of bigotry: all are the same as a few.

6. What message does homonaturality send to our young people?

It depends on what you think homonaturality is. If you regard it as perversion, then you'll convey that to the young people you address. However, if you are able to separate perversion from integrity and give sexual orientation its true value, then the message will be: "Be true to yourself while trying to be moral, responsible, and self-less." Here's a surprise for you: our Christian young people are way ahead of the rest of us when it comes to dealing with homonaturality. If you condemn it, you might just send the message that you're out of touch with reality.

7. Marriage has always been between one man and one woman.

Wrong!! Polygamy had been the law of the land on this planet for as long as monogamy. Using slaves to ensure offspring had been in effect for almost as long. The ideal of men and women choosing their own life-partners is less than 200 years old. The concept of women having any rights in marriage is even newer. And the idea of inter-racial marriage is the newest of all. Marriage has not always been between one man and one woman.

8. The homonatural lifestyle is all about promiscuity.

Promiscuity is perpetuated where a society denies protection and acknowledgment to a segment of its community. The word "lifestyle" is a negative generalization of an entire group for the behavior of only some of its members. Then the non-offending portion of that group is forced to carry the stigma of something for which they are not guilty.

9. Homosexuality is not natural.

If 'natural' is determined by the ability to sire offspring, then the statement could be true. If 'natural' means the fitting together of male and female organs, then the statement might be true also. But why do many heterosexual couples use intercourse techniques usually ascribed to gays and lesbians? However, if 'natural' refers to how one responds to sexual attraction, then the statement is definitely not true.

10. <u>Marriage is reserved for bearing children</u>

It used to be so when the bearing of offspring was crucial to a society's survival. But today over-population threatens most nations and marriage without children is something to be admired, not ridiculed.

11. <u>The Gay Agenda</u>

The Gay Agenda is not to secure special rights, but to restore fairness and legal protection to a group that some people want to exclude from basic human rights. Until you have been stopped at the hospital entrance and prevented from being at the bedside of a dying loved one because you're not related or married, you won't understand the pain and anger of rejection. Until you get fired or evicted because of a judgmental label, you won't understand 'gay rights.' Until you see biological family steal personal belongings that your special other intended for you as his/her love-partner, you won't understand what the Gay Agenda is all about.

CHAPTER 16

•❈•

THREAT TO MARRIAGE? PROVE IT!!

The next time I hear people say that homonaturality is a threat to marriage and family values, I'm not going to let them get away with just saying those words and then walking away. I'm going to ask them to describe how these two ideals are actually endangered by a non-heteronatural orientation. They won't be able to throw out those quick unsubstantiated sound bites like some campaigning politician and then walk off with the protective cloak of innuendo. I want to know in black and white how a homonatural person poses any menace to marriage or family values.

What can they say? *Will it be claimed that homonaturals want to alter the customary number of people who can get married?* Maybe they feel that gays and lesbians want to re-institute polygamy so their promiscuous tendencies can be satisfied legally. Maybe they are afraid that heteronaturals will be the only ones who believe that marriage is reserved for two people who want to dedicate themselves to the well-being of one another.

Will it be alleged that homonaturals have some motivation other than love and commitment for wanting to be married? Maybe they can't imagine homonaturals being capable of faithfulness, loyalty, selflessness, or sacrificial love. Maybe they see only 'sex' in the word homosexual. Considering the frequency of adultery and divorce among heteronaturals, one might ask, "Isn't sex the main motivator of these problems?" Do heteronatural people ever get married for reasons other than love and commitment? What about heteronatural persons who use marriage to promote political and career-related alliances? What about rural households who beget children just to have enough labor on the farm?

Do they think that homonaturals are just using marriage as a ploy to become legally qualified to adopt children whom they can then convert to their lifestyle? Do you really believe that such an appetite would be content with the limited number of prospects adoption might provide? Why would people determined to be so devious put themselves into a position of such legal scrutiny, restriction and responsibility? Not a very bright plan, is it?

The real threat to marriage and family values

What would you call a group of people (otherwise known as fundamentalists) who reward their leaders for remaining ignorant and fearful? Imagine how much money flows into the coffers of fundamentalist evangelists just for not permitting the developing science of sexual orientation to affect traditional theology. Consider the false affirmation given to preachers, priests, and rabbis who keep the homonatural problem at arms length, never letting it become a matter

⟫ 53 ⟪

of importance in their theology or worship. Think about this: gay persons are more positively regarded if they keeps their orientations secret, even pretending to be heteronatural. To be dishonest is more desirable than to be true to one's own integrity. Don't ask, don't tell, and there's no limit to how high one can rise in life. But try to be honest and sincere; then watch your future evaporate. Is there something wrong with this picture?

What would you call persons who would rather hurt other people than get to know them? Who would rather wear spiritual blinders than to be receptive to evolving knowledge about how people are wired? Who would rather throw the baby out with the bath water than to admit that the baby was even in the tub? What would you call a group of people who would rather deny a feared group the right to marry or adopt children than try to understand how they tick? Wouldn't you call **them** a threat to marriage and family values?

CHAPTER 17

FAMILY VALUES

Lack of family values is a criticism often leveled against gay and lesbian persons who want to become parents. It is argued that homonaturals are unable to attain the same parenting ideals that heteronatural people do. However when critics are pinned down as to what these family values are, it usually turns out that they're not talking about 'values' at all. Values are long-lasting principles that don't change as societies evolve, such as honesty, decency, loyalty, safety, or love. What they're really defending are more temporary, culture-bound 'rules' that they want to perpetuate, such as one mother/one father as the only ideal parenting model.

Isn't it ironic that the defenders of 'family values' in such situations, then, are the ones really violating values like honesty and integrity when they use general words to conceal very specific prejudices? One mother/one father is not a universal, timeless value. It is a modern interpretation of family organization that has not always been the norm. Ancient households were considered healthy and normal when polygamy was being practiced, when slaves nursed and nurtured the young of their masters, and when any family elder was regarded as having authority over fully grown children.

One mother/one father is just another rule that fits the time we live in, that reflects what the majority practice, but which has no more claim to eternal normality than did Levirate marriage in Bible times (see chart at the end of this chapter). In each age, fundamentalists have held up their 'rules' as the absolute authority for human conduct, even using scripture to prove their right to do so. But every age has evolved to adopt its own separate and distinctive way of looking at things.

What makes some people so sure the Bible must be taken literally?

While "faith is being sure of what we hope for and certain of what we do not see" (Heb. 11:1), 'faith' is often also the defender of what we cannot give up. While faith is supposed to be married to truth, it more often becomes the mistress of tradition. Protecting what we're comfortable with usually takes precedence over what makes us uncomfortable.

Fundamentalists are faithful people who have let their literalist outlook corrupt the gradual way God often lets himself be revealed to his people. This revelation comes about through changes in customs, new discoveries, inventions, and the evolution of language. Anyone in any age who believes that only the current language and tradition matches God's will for his people is a fundamentalist and such a person is out of touch with the 'flow' of God's truth.

History needs to be studied and appreciated for the contributions each society has made toward understanding God's will. What was normal for one age is not necessarily the norm for successive societies.

Is "Family Values" being used as a weapon?

Some fundamentalist religions use the idea of 'family values' as a club to inflict judgment and guilt upon persons whose lifestyles don't conform to their view of decency. Either they assign a negative label to conduct they might not understand or they lump all persons with a single characteristic together ignoring that only a few within that group actually express the conduct in a way of which they disapprove.

If such groups would only limit their evaluations to the principles of decency listed in the first paragraph of this article, their condemnation might be less offensive. But they choose to include rules of behavior that are less constant than principles, moral regulations that change from era to era. The chart on the last page of this chapter lists some changes that have happened over the centuries. These 'rules' of evolving societies would have been blindly defended in their respective ages as being absolute, unchallengeable, and the embodiment of eternal truth.

Ask yourself what customs within your own lifetime could be added to this list that show how attitudes changed over the years from what was once considered immoral to what today is thought of as just ordinary and normal. Maybe it was the way your ancestors used to dress and how they demanded that others behave the same way. Maybe certain kinds of entertainment were taboo back then, but now are perfectly innocent. Maybe times have changed regarding food you eat, transportation you use, radio programs you listen to, movies you go to, what days you work, or the way you cut your hair.

Sexuality is the most recent frontier

'Decency' is a cornerstone principle of faithfulness and rules of sexuality are so engrained in decency that people let them take on the same importance as the principle itself. Of all the rules mankind has sought to impose on human behavior, those governing sexual identity and conduct have probably been the ones most strongly enforced. And among those rules about sexuality, the rules about homonaturality have been the ones most fiercely and most selfishly maintained.

Ironically, openness to discussing these rules has traditionally been so stifled that most modern societies have chosen not to explore what aspects of sexuality might actually be healthy and favored in God's eyes. The positions on sexuality adopted by most modern societies have been based on what makes them comfortable, not on what might please a loving creator.

If a sexual activity does not demand, does not seize without invitation, or does not abuse a relationship, it may be said to conform to Godly intent. Until people learn how to tell the difference between eternal principles and human rules, we will continue to make the fundamentalist error of supposing the latter to be as important as the former. At that point, their 'family values' will have become valueless.

Notice the chart on the next page that illustrates how far societies have progressed in changing 'rules' of morality. Applying modern rules on the basis of tradition is really narrow-minded selective judgment.

ANCIENT NORMS	MODERN NORMS
Eldest male rules household	Household owner is leader
Male parent rules adult son	Parent is advisor of adult son
Female is property, not person	Female is person, not property
Non-virgin female is worthless	All females have value
Wife/woman has few rights	Wife/woman has rights
Babies can be thrown away	Children must be protected
Elders decide marriages	Individuals decide marriages
Polygamy practical/approved	Monogamy required
Concubine acceptable	Unfaithfulness disapproved
Levirate marriage acceptable (brother of deceased weds sister-in-law & fathers children by her for him)	Violates laws of monogamy
Slavery is normal/ sex is okay Slave family can be split apart Breeding of slaves acceptable	Slavery immoral & illegal
Males control divorce laws	Women & children protected
Male adultery is only against the wife/betrothed of another man, not with an unmarried woman	Adultery is immoral, but often ignored if not brazen; (being in love often cited for forgiveness)

CHAPTER 18

❋

LETS JUST AGREE TO DISAGREE

A Tongue-in-Cheek Confession

We are also guilty of stereo-typing

When my wife and I became aware that we had a gay son, we quickly identified with what it means to be a victim of malicious ridicule and of moral and spiritual condemnation. Because we knew our son had faith, values, and character incompatible with the kind of life his critics imagined him to be living, it hurt us so much that they were willing to condemn him without even knowing him. As we continued to learn about homonaturality and the ways that it mirrors all the good and bad in heteronaturality, it was not difficult for us to appreciate how easy it is for others to throw all homonatural people into a faceless group and treat them as if all of them were guilty of error that only some of them commit.

I know it's easy to be so narrow-minded because I've done it myself. Those of us who defend homonaturality and our gay and lesbian loved ones are also guilty of stereotypical ignorance and arrogance. We tend to group together all persons who are opposed to homonaturality and give them a single negative label: homophobic. That word expresses all we want to consider as we vent our anger and frustration toward that group. We tend to ignore the individuality of real people and to focus on the similarity of what we think they represent. We don't want to see them as real people with understandable concerns because if we forced ourselves to recognize persons with names and faces, it would create a terrible conflict between what we think we know about homophobia and the personalities of the people standing before us.

You don't deserve to be ridiculed

You who oppose homonaturality do not deserve to have your individual attitudes and convictions lumped together with other persons' outlooks that might be either more extreme or less committed than yours. Each of us is unique and our perspective deserves individual appreciation. No one can really know you until they have spoken to you, listened to you, and gotten to know you somewhat.

There are those of you who have given a lot of thought and investigation to homonaturality. You have prayed about it. You have studied your Bibles. You have honestly and faithfully come to the conclusion that your opposition to homonaturality is God-favored and in line with scholarly opinion on the matter. It would be an insult to your integrity and spiritual conviction to be compared to someone that is against homonaturality based on no effort of their own to try to discern what is true and acceptable.

However, some people do oppose homonaturality not because they've thought it through but just because that's what is expected of them. Their families, their churches, their teachers, or their peers have labeled what they believe to be unacceptable behavior and many people are willing to just accept that guidance as well-intentioned and probably correct. Such people should not be thrown into a melting pot with those who have seriously studied the problem of homonaturality or with those for whom the height of their intellectual accomplishment is only as high as a bar stool.

Others may have been first hand observers of inappropriate behavior that they believe to be typical of a certain type of perverted person. Maybe it happened in a public bathroom, a theatre, or in a park where their children were playing nearby. The offense given to them may have been so unnerving and so unwelcome that their discomfort should not be put alongside of the opinions of people who have never ever experienced a similar intrusion of privacy.

Questions I have to ask myself

How can I oppose someone I don't even know? Is it acceptable for me to put a person I don't know into a generalized group and then say 'I know all I need to know about him or her? I've done just that. Just let me hear which denomination you belong to and I can quickly assign you an image and a personality that your closest friends and family members wouldn't recognize. Just say 'we hate the sin, but love the sinner' and my mind will file you away to a place of meaningless conformity to all the other people I don't want to understand or get to know. It's easier to deal with you when I don't have to meet or speak directly to you.

Why do I keep rambling on and on if I recognize this problem of stereotyping. Why don't I put forth more effort to stop being like that? Could it be just for that reason—that it requires EFFORT to change how I feel about people? I think that's exactly why I don't change. I'm lazy and self-satisfied. I don't really want to get to know you; if I did, wouldn't I soon realize that I could be wrong?

A possible solution

I know what we can do. Let's just agree to disagree. I need you to keep on being the nameless, faceless person you are so I won't have to take any responsibility for my ignorance and arrogance. You stay on your side of the tracks and I'll stay on mine. We'll shout back and forth at one another, but let's agree that we won't ever try to get to know one another, okay? Who in their right mind would want to go that far?

> "It is with narrow-souled people as with narrow-necked bottles: the less they have in them the more noise they make in pouring it out."—Alexander Pope

> "Shallow understanding from people of good will is more frustrating than absolute misunderstanding from people of ill will."—Martin Luther King, Jr.

> "What else is love but understanding and rejoicing in the fact that another person lives, acts, and experiences otherwise than we do and crosswise to our purposes?

For love to bridge these opposites through joy it must not eliminate or deny them.—Even self-love presupposes an irreconcilable duality (or multiplicity) in a single person."—Frederick Nietzsche

"Understanding the spirit of our institutions to aim at the elevation of man, I am opposed to whatever tends to degrade them."—Abraham Lincoln

"If all mankind minus one were of one opinion, mankind would be no more justified in silencing that one person than he, if he had the power, would be justified in silencing mankind."—John Stuart Mill

"Evil acts of the past are never rectified by evil acts of the present." (*Lyndon Johnson*, Statement on riots in New York City, New York, July 21, 1964)

"We have learned that social injustice is the destruction of justice itself." (*Herbert Hoover, American Individualism*, 1922)

"The war is over—the rebels are our countrymen again." (*Ulysses Grant*, April 9, 1865) [Comments to his cheering men after Lee's surrender ending the U.S. Civil War.]

CHAPTER 19

───•❈•───

HOW CAN I PERSUADE YOU?

The Problem

What can I say to persuade you that homonaturality is not what you think it is? You have a firm opinion about homonaturality and it's probably 100% negative. I understand where you're coming from. I also once thought that all homonaturals were perverts, not to be trusted around young people, and definitely worthy of all the condemnation they receive.

Then I found out I have a gay son. Even though I eventually became convinced that he truly was a homonatural by nature and didn't just choose to be one, I still had to resolve a conflict in my mind between what I thought I knew about homonaturality and the obviously faithful and moral character of my son. I couldn't just say that because he likes boys better than he does girls that all the qualities he displays are phony. Just because this one part of his nature is at odds with what most people consider normal, I couldn't throw away my certainty that John is a good person.

So, I have embarked on a quest to learn as much as I can about homonaturality: what the Bible says about it, what science says about it, and what people in general believe about it. I started looking at history, at ways our ancestors dealt with new ideas that most people then considered immoral until they eventually were 'proven' to not be as threatening as they first thought. I also opened myself up to the possibility that I could be wrong about what I have believed for years. I dared to become acquainted with other homonatural people and with their parents, family members, and friends who loved them and stood by them. It seemed important to find out why they didn't choose to draw a line in the sand between themselves and the ones they loved.

The Solution

What I have come to learn is so simple and yet so difficult for many to accept. To get to where I am on this subject, you'll have to make a few concessions. Let me tell you what they are and then see if you think the risk of keeping a relationship alive between you and your loved ones who say they're gay is worth the gamble.

First, we must acknowledge that in every age of history discoveries emerge which contradict the prevailing knowledge about many subjects.

Second, because of this fact, no society can be fully certain that they know all there is to know on a particular subject.

Third (and this may be the most difficult for you), you cannot always accept the literal, apparently plain-sense meaning of modern English words in the Bible.

Fourth, one cannot superimpose modern understanding on ancient practices.

Fifth, when we remember that the Bible has been misinterpreted and misapplied in various ways in the past to defend erroneous views and attitudes, we must acknowledge that it will happen again in the future, and may be happening right now.

And lastly, we cannot ignore the fact that the church is historically the last institution to affirm new discoveries.

My Reasoning

In which areas of human knowledge has there been one constant view from the beginning of history until now? Religion? Nope. Science? Definitely not. How societies organize themselves? Not at all. There is no human effort that has not undergone change, reform, improvement, or refinement. Everything evolves from the primitive to the complex. It's a fact of life.

It is my belief that humanity of ancient times could not, for example, have conceived of 'brain waves,' the electrical movement of nerve impulses that command the organs, limbs, and senses of the body to function and move. What we know now about such things is far more than they knew, but probably nowhere near what mankind will know 100 years from now. No one with any maturity doubts this, right?

The ancients (from O.T. times through the Middle Ages) thought, talked, and behaved almost completely in response to the uncertainty of life with superstition and fear. They fortified their ignorance with rigid traditionalism. As was mentioned previously on page 42 of this book, when God revealed himself to the ancients, He did so within the limits of what they knew or could imagine. When the ax head floated in 2 Kings 6:6, it was within the confines of current knowledge because people knew that some things do float. Although Elisha's act contradicted a known principle that iron does not float, It would have been so far outside the limits of current imagination if he had caused the axe head to hover in the air or to disappear, reappearing on the shore.

God's revelations about himself come in varying portions at different times in history when his people are ready to witness His 'sameness' in new ways.

What am I leading up to? Just this: man's knowledge about sexuality has also evolved from the primitive to the complex. Early man didn't know about ovulation and impregnation; he just believed the woman provided a space of incubation, not contributing anything to the formation of a baby. Menstrual cycles at one time in Hebrew history were periods (no pun intended) of uncleanness that brought severe moral punishment when ignored; today it's just an inconvenience. Babies born female were not as desirable as male offspring and could just be thrown away like so much garbage.

When the ancients thought about sexual relationships, they differentiated between good relationships and bad ones. Both were only between a man and a woman. They had words that distinguished the good (marriage, love, duty) from the bad (prostitution, adultery, incest). I'm confident that the ancients had no concept whatever of same-gender attraction and affection as a wholesome, natural fact of human nature. Therefore they had only one description of it and the label was 100% negative. heteronatural conduct was understandably dual, but homonatural behavior was considered singularly unholy.

This is the view of homonaturality that has persisted for thousands of years. Now, we're seeing the proposition that maybe humans do have more than one orientation. No, it has not been proven to be the case, but the evidence is building. We know this to be true because more and more people, many of whom are conscientious Christians, are coming to a point of acceptance just because they believe the information they're receiving from outside the church is more trust-worthy than the rigidity of the traditional Biblical position. When sexual orientation is finally accepted as an undeniable fact of human nature, the church will conform its teachings in the same reluctant and belated way it did when the flatness of the earth was disproved, when slavery was acknowledged as immoral, when women were granted equality with men, and when life is created by human beings (just around the corner in science.

Words used in the Bible to signify an immoral relationship between a man and a woman are easy to recognize, because there also are words to describe a moral one. With homonaturality, the Bible writers and translators have been content to use the same word for all same-gender intimate relationships, assuming them to all be unacceptable. But the time is ripe for linguists to coin new words to describe same-gender relationships that are also either wholesome or perverse. homonaturality is just like heteronaturality. in that both are natural even though one is more prevalent. Both have elements that are moral and immoral, healthy and unhealthy, natural and unnatural. homonaturality is not what you always thought it was. You may not believe that now and you might never come to accept it. But when it is finally acknowledged as a natural and potentially wholesome activity, you may be remembered by your descendants as a person who wore spiritual shackles, keeping one foot in the dark and ignorant past. They will probably forgive you, but don't you think you will still be somewhat of a disappointment to them?

CHAPTER 20

---•❈•---

IS IT POSSIBLE TO BE BOTH GAY AND CHRISTIAN?

This chapter is an outline of an oral presentation made at the Shenandoah Valley Gay & Lesbian Association (SVGLA) in Harrisonburg, VA, on September 2, 2002. My purpose at that meeting was to reach out to any homonatural person who either (1) felt alienated from his/her church because of sexual orientation or (2) might be on a spiritual quest for understanding how the Bible speaks to sexual orientation. Not surprisingly, many in the group did feel estranged from church life and had no desire to renew it. Generally they were civil and attentive to my appeal, but I left feeling that much more needed to be done if the gospel was to have any meaningful significance for them.

It is my hope that this outline will stimulate self-examination and eventual discussion. It is divided into three sections, two of which flow out of the first. The 3 sections are:

1. True or False statements about the Bible and homonaturality

2. Question: How many 'bomb-shells' are there in the homophobic's cannon?

3. Question: What is the homonatural's most effective method of coping with homophobia?

TRUE OR FALSE

1. T or F? Any homonatural person who wants to claim a relationship to the God of the Bible should not fear any of the language scripture contains regarding same-gender intimacy.

   A. <u>True</u>—because Bible writers had no concept of sexual orientation in their time. This means they condemned heteronatural persons for going against their orientation.

   B. <u>False</u>—if the Bible is used unfairly or erroneously as a weapon of criticism ("we hate the sin, but we love the sinner").

C. <u>True</u>—because God would not author a writing that opposes a creature he has created.

2. T or F? Any homonatural person who claims to be a Christian can find in the Bible what is expected of him/her concerning faithful sexuality.

   A. <u>False</u>—if the seeker only uses the word 'sex' to search scripture.
   B. <u>True</u>—because sexuality isn't just about sex; it is more about affection and consideration, and sometimes abuse.

3. T or F? Any homonatural person who is trying to live a Christian life can live any way he/she wants and still be regarded as faithful.

   A. <u>True</u>—if the emphasis is always placed on the word 'trying'.
   B. <u>False</u>—if the emphasis is placed on 'wants'.

4. T or F? Either the Bible should be interpreted literally or it has no authority.

   A. <u>True</u>—if you appreciate the influence of history and culture on scripture.
   B. <u>False</u>—if you minimize the influence of history and culture on scripture.

How many arguments are there in our critics' arsenal?

1. Scriptural weapons:

   A. Misinterpreted 'clobber passages'

      (1) O.T. holiness codes
      (2) non-scriptural interpretation of Sodom story
      (3) non-contextual analysis of Romans 1
      (4) non-universal assignment of English word to vague Greek term

   B. Misapplied inferences of non-related passages

      (1) Adam & Eve, not Adam & Steve—actually more like Andrew & Esther
      (2) "Go and sin no more."
      (3) literalism
      (4) ignoring grace; over-emphasizing la

2. Non-scriptural weapons:

   A. Family values argument

      B. Unnatural intercourse can't produce offspring
      C. Orientation is a choice
      D. homonaturality is always perverse, never wholesome

E.   At best, homonaturality is a mental/physical defect

F.   homonaturals gave us AIDS.

What is the homonatural's most effective way of coping with opposition?

1.   Do you want to confront and persuade?

   A. Faith-oriented

      (1)   study and pray
      (2)   interpret scripture consistently
      (3)   respond with positive passages
      (4)   utilize lessons from church history (gentiles, leprosy)
      (5)   demonstrate flip-flops of church tradition
      (6)   emphasize grace, not law
      (7)   emphasize love, not judgment

   B. Secular

      (1)   research and study
      (2)   demonstrate evolution of knowledge
      (3)   quote latest positions of reputable entities
      (4)   demand safety and respect

2. Or do you just want to co-exist?

   A. Find your groove—in or out

      (1)   live your life
      (2)   follow path of least resistance

   B. Protect yourself legally

      (1) obtain power of attorney and living will
      (2)   put property and accounts under joint ownership
      (3)   carry signed notices naming emergency contacts
      (4)   designate beneficiaries on your insurance and 401k

   C. Establish community

      (1)   religious
      (2)   service & good will
      (3)   interact with straight persons
      (4)   be a good example
      (5)   stay positive

CHAPTER 21

---•❋•---

THOUGHT READER

This is the story of a remarkable and kindly old man named Jezeriah who had the ability to know if a person's thoughts matched the words being spoken. If the speaker was thinking hurtful thoughts while saying seemingly positive words, Jezeriah would know. On the positive side, he also could tell when a person's words were sincere, whether they came from a strong faith, or maybe even from God himself. Jezeriah's "thought reading" was not something he openly announced; he just preferred to be a listener more than a teller.

How did he do it? Eyeglasses! Jezeriah had special glasses that enabled him to see people's breath when they talked. After many years of studying and testing his unusual skill, he came to learn that certain colors of people's breath generally represented different kinds of emotion. He would watch people's breath through his eyeglasses and would see that their words changed color as the speakers moved from subject to subject.

Follow this chart and try to decipher the thoughts of each person as they speak. Ask yourself, which person is being more honest?

Red	=	anger	Pink	=	happiness
Green	=	jealousy	Aqua	=	contentedness
Yellow	=	fear	Orange	=	courage
Brown	=	lying	Purple	=	truth
Black	=	hate	Blue	=	love

Here is how one brief speech by a preacher appeared to Jezeriah:

(brown>) "I don't have many material things, (yellow>) but I don't need much. (red>) What's most important to me is that people respect one another, (green>) no matter how much money they have."

Here are the same words Jezeriah heard from a homeless man:

(purple>) "I don't have many material things, (aqua>) but I don't need much. (blue>) What's important to me is that people respect one another, (orange>) no matter how much money they have."

Now if you or I heard these words, would we understand them the same as Jezeriah does? I doubt it.

How would you talk if you knew someone was reading your breath? Well, one day Jezeriah happened to be in a church with a friend attending a church council meeting. As he listened to the speakers, he put on his special glasses.

An older member stood up and started explaining why homonatural people should not be welcomed into the church.

(brown>) "Everyone knows (purple>) that God does not approve (yellow) of the homonatural lifestyle. (red>) We can't have (purple>) people in our church who refuse to repent (red>) and just want to keep on doing their thing."

Another person asked to be recognized and then said, *(purple>) "We have to protect our children. (red>) homonaturals are out to seduce our young men and (yellow>) recruit them into the lifestyle."*

Did Jezeriah have a problem? Even though the speakers were saying things that he found objectionable, their breath showed that they were speaking from a sincere faith. They actually believed the things they were saying. How could he tell if what a person was saying was not God-favored even though the person, himself, believed it to be so?

It was not hard. Whenever a person spoke words that were God-favored, their colored breath would start to rise upwards as it left the person's lips. But if what they were saying was not God-favored, their breath immediately started dropping toward the ground. So even when the two church council members seemed to be talking from their faith, their words were utterances that God would rather have not heard from them.

So Jezeriah asked his friend if the council would let a visitor speak. When he was acknowledged, Jerzeriah stood up and thanked the council for letting him address them. As he spoke, Jezeriah watched his own breath come out of his mouth and rise toward the ceiling. "Ladies and Gentlemen, I know that both speakers this evening spoke from their hearts and that they really believe that gays and lesbians are not in God's favor." As Jezeriah paused he looked directly into the eyes of each speaker as he continued. "Sir," he said to the first speaker, "you are a man of faith, but your faith is caught up in anger and fear more than it is in knowledge." The older man said nothing because he couldn't deny Jezeriah's words.

Jezeriah looked just as intently at the 2nd speaker. "You also, sir, are both as angry and as afraid as you are sincere. Let me ask you both a question to get you to think about homonaturality in a different way. "Do you believe that the ancients knew as much as we do about diseases? Knowing that you would say 'no,' I suggest that there are many areas of modern knowledge that the ancients could not even imagine in their wildest dreams. Things like space travel, organ transplants, or DNA." The council members seemed to be under a spell. They remained silent.

Jezeriah continued. "If ancient Bible writers were not as aware of things as we are, they could only have written within the understanding that they did have. I fear that too many people today would like to think that the ancients understood what we understand, but we know that couldn't have been possible. So we need to remember that the things they did say conformed to their limited knowledge."

Jezeriah paused to catch his breath, but no one spoke up. "Let me ask you another question about heteronaturality. Is there a difference between how a heteronatural person is attracted to another human being and what he or she does about it?"

The older council member replied, "Yes, of course there is. Everybody knows that to be so."

"Then," asked Jezeriah, "why do we automatically assume that it is not the case for a homonatural person? Isn't what he understands and what he does two different things? Of course they are. The bigger question is, 'Could God disapprove of what he does while approving of what he understands?' I believe God does disapprove of promiscuity between persons who have no long-term interest in one another, but I also believe that He approves of a homonatural wanting to be in a long-term relationship, wanting to be able to commit himself to another's well-being, wanting to lift up another higher than himself. That's called LOVE, and we know that 'God IS Love,', right?"

Still no one dared to speak. They were caught off guard by Jezeriah's eloquence.

He continued, "I agree that the behavior Leviticus describes and the behavior that Paul describes in Romans and other chapters is the kind of conduct that God definitely does not approve of. And if we knew that a person insisted on living that kind of a lifestyle, we would be right in opposing it. But God does not disapprove of love if it really is love, no matter whether it is between heteronaturals or homonaturals. Today we are finding our understanding of homonatural orientation as being just like heteronaturality when it comes to love. And it's also the same as heteronaturality when it comes to selfishness and abuse. Either orientation is capable of both good and bad behavior. The Bible does speak against idolatry, abuse, and self-servedness, but it cannot be interpreted to be against worship, love, and self-sacrifice. So if a homonatural can achieve those positive qualities by being himself, who is to say God is against such an accomplishment?"

How did the church council reply? How would you reply?

CHAPTER 22

— ⟐ —

GOBBLE-D-GUCK

A Story of Misinformation & Tolerance

<u>Characters</u>

Narrator   Henry   Martha   Jason   Susie

Narrator: Henry and Martha have been married for 40 years. They have lived in their neighborhood for 20 years. All the houses on their street look almost alike. There are different colors, different landscapes, and different cars in the driveways, but the houses have a similarity that's easy to recognize. One day Henry looks out a window of his house and sees a bulldozer being unloaded at the vacant lot next door.

Henry: Martha, it looks like we're going to have a new neighbor. This is great. Now that we're retired and have lots of time on our hands, it'll be fun to sit on our porch and watch the progress of the work going on next door.

Narrator: So each day Henry goes out on his enclosed air-conditioned porch, relaxes in his lounge chair with his fresh ice tea, paper, pencils, and binoculars nearby. He yells out to Martha about each new phase of the building project. She usually never answers because she understands Henry's need just to be talking, not necessarily to be heard.

Henry: Martha! They're starting the foundation. Same blocks as ours. Same mortar mix. But it sure is an unusual layout. Don't think I've ever seen a floor plan like that before.

Henry: Martha! The walls are going up. Same lumber as ours. Same studs. Same plywood sheeting. But look at all those windows. I guess they won't mind having everyone know their business.

Henry:	Martha! They got the roof on. Same rafter and joist spacing as ours. Same plywood again. Even the same shingles. But how about those gables and projections. Wow, that's different. Those guys really know what they're doing. We couldn't live in a house like that, but, oh well, different strokes for different folks.
Henry:	Martha! The insulation crew is here. This will be boring. If you've seen one kind of insulation, you've seen them all. Ho, hum—(pause, and then yelling)—Hey, wait a second. Martha! Martha!! Martha!!!. Come out here, quick!! Martha, are you listening to me. Get out here right now!!
Martha:	What are you getting so excited about, Henry?
Henry:	Look at what they're doing. I can't believe it. Look at what kind of insulation they're putting in those walls. It's not like our Pink-N-Puffy. Oh, my goodness. This is terrible. This is really bad. Martha! Somebody has to warn them. They're installing Gobble-D-Guck. What will our other neighbors think?
Narrator:	Henry spills his iced tea, drops his binoculars, and stumbles over his chair as he rushes off his porch yelling and screaming at the insulation crew, shouting for them to stop immediately, and to go get the building foreman.
Henry:	Stop! Stop! You can't put that stuff in there. Haven't you heard about that evil junk? Where are you brains? Whose idea was this? Find me someone to talk to! I've got to warn them! This is disaster, big time!!
Jason:	Hi. My name is Jason. This is my partner, Jim. We're going to be your new neighbors. That's all the fuss about?
Henry:	Glad to meet you Jason. Jim. I'm Henry; this is my wife, Martha. Listen, do you guys know what you're doing? Hasn't anyone told you about Gob . . . Gobble . . . Gobble-D-Guck?
Jason:	I think I know what you're going to say. You use Pink-n-Puffy, right?
Henry:	Well, yes. Everybody around here does. It's the only safe kind of insulation there is. We've all learned since we were kids what Gobble-D-Guck does to a house, even to a neighborhood if it is allowed to stay. That stuff is wicked. My builder said that as far as insulation goes, that stuff is abomination. It doesn't even come in bundles like Pink-N-Puffy. It gets blown into the wall as a liquid and then it hardens in there. It's an abomination and it's definitely not natural.
Jason:	Henry! Henry! Relax. Let me show you something. Here; read this label that came with Gobble-D-Good. Go ahead; read it out loud. What does it say?

Henry: (reading) "Attention, consumer: this product is safe and efficient. Recent scientific advancement has discovered that the dreaded Gobble-D-Guck actually has two ingredients: the bad one we've always known about and a secret good ingredient, one that's been hidden for thousands of years. Our scientists have found a way to unlock the good ingredient and to deactivate the bad one. The result is Gobble-D-Good, the product you're holding now. We apologize for the confusion over our product's name, but we believe in naming something for what it is, not for what it is not. Gobble-D-Good "gobbles" up discomfort and we think that's good. Thank you for using our product."

Jason: So, you see, Henry. You have nothing to fear. We can live with this product if we can just trust this new modification of an old idea. It doesn't have to be like it's always been. It's possible to improve on something and make it better and safer and even desirable for some folks. Pink-N-Puffy is still a good product and is probably best for lots of people, but Gobble-D-Good is what we like and it's what we intend to go with.

Henry: I don't know, Jason. It's hard to let go of old fears. My dad told me about Gobble-D-Guck; his dad told him. As far back as any of us can remember, no one has ever had anything good to say about Gobble-D-Guck. It's something that's been handed down for generations. If they saw the danger in Gobble-D-Guck, who are we to try to see it as something different? We don't want our house ruined and our property values to plummet.

Jason: Listen, Henry. Give it a chance. Wait 10 years. If our house shows signs of deterioration due to Gobble-D-Good, we'll tear the house down and move away. Is that fair enough?

Henry: Well, I don't want to wait that long. I'll give you one year. If that stuff is as bad as I think it is, 12 months will be long enough to prove it.

Jason: Thanks, Henry. In the meantime, we'll do our best to be good neighbors to you and Martha even though this one part of who we are is hard for you to accept.

Narrator: One year later, Henry is in his living room when the doorbell rings.

Martha: Henry, would you see who is at the door?

Henry: Hello girls; what can we do for you.

Susie: Hi; we're Susie and Sally. We're going to be your new neighbors across the street. We're building a house just like the beautiful one next to you.

Henry: Don't tell me. I bet you plan to use Gobble-D-Good in the walls, right?

<u>Susie:</u>   How did you know?

<u>Henry:</u>   Oh, it was just a hunch. Welcome to the neighborhood. We hope you and Sally will be very happy.

CHAPTER 23

THE SCRIBE AND THE PHARISEE

PHARISEE: Let's create an apparent negative future condition.

SCRIBE: What do you mean?

PHARISEE: Suppose we define a human characteristic that won't be completely understood for at least 2000 years, but which, when it is close to being understood will mistakenly be called bad because it's similar to something we already know is bad.

SCRIBE: What will it be called?

PHARISEE: We don't know yet. How can you name something no one has identified. Most likely it will have the same name as the thing we are observing now, but that will confuse people and make it difficult for them to see it as different.

SCRIBE: Is it possible that we're experiencing it now even though we can't identify it?

PHARISEE: Well, sure; but like I said, if it's here, we probably have lumped it together with something very similar to it, probably something as bad as it is mysterious.

SCRIBE: Do we know anything at all about it?

PHARISEE: Well, there are opinions floating around about it, but who can know which one of them, if any, will survive the test of time and will it even describe it accurately then?

SCRIBE: This is confusing.

PHARISEE: Yes, I know it is, but don't we have a duty to mankind to clearly state today what future evil will develop so those people in the next millennium will have definite proof that it's wrong?

SCRIBE: So, won't this require a generation-by-generation, intensive, hands-on manipulation of what we do know so that what we don't know won't surprise us when we finally do know it?

PHARISEE: Now you're confusing me.

SCRIBE: No, I think I'm figuring it out. Listen, all we have to do is talk about it, write about it, share it in our fellowship, and above all, teach it to our children.

PHARISEE: Teach what?

SCRIBE: That someday something contained in what we now know to be bad might try to call itself good.

PHARISEE: But, what if that something actually is something good?

SCRIBE: We can't afford to take any chances. Better to sacrifice a few good things than to surrender control of what we already know and accept as bad. Why rock the boat?

PHARISEE: Okay, I think I understand what you mean?

SCRIBE: NO, NO, NO !! THAT WILL BE THE BIGGEST PROBLEM OF ALL. DON'T EVER, EVER SAY, "I UNDERSTAND WHAT YOU MEAN." DO YOU WANT TO RUIN IT FOR THE REST OF US, ESPECIALLY THOSE LIKE US 2000 YEARS FROM NOW?

Chapter 24

ADAM AND STEVE

ADAM: Hi, my name is Adam.

STEVE: Hi, my name is Steve.

ADAM: You don't look like a Steve.

STEVE: Do you always judge a book by It's cover?

ADAM: Everybody knows that Steve's are . . . are . . . well, they're different.

STEVE: I can assure you. I am definitely a Steve.

ADAM: You don't act like a Steve.

STEVE: Here we go again. How am I supposed to act?

ADAM: Well, I've been told, or . . . that is, my experience tells me . . . hey, everybody knows that Steve's do things differently.

STEVE: Is that good or bad?

ADAM: Well, bad, obviously. I'll have you know that I've been properly instructed by my church elders about good and bad. And since I know everything worth knowing and that there is nothing new for me to be instructed about, anything that comes up for the first time has to be bad, especially if it conflicts with something the elders consider unquestionable.

STEVE: Okay, then tell me everything you know.

ADAM: Everything? All of it? Right now?

STEVE: Yes, do you have anything else to do right now?

ADAM: Well, I was told to stand here and try to not get into any trouble. But I don't have time to list everything.

STEVE: Okay, then just tell me the 2 most important things.

ADAM: The 2 most important things? Okay, that's easy enough. Rule #1: NEVER CONTRADICT RELIGIOUS INSTRUCTION. Rule #2: If something new appears, follow rule #1.

STEVE: Fine. Now let me ask you a question: are you seeing anyone special right now?

ADAM: Well . . . ah . . . er . . . I'm not sure, but I have a feeling I will be in the very near future.

CHAPTER 25

PLAIN TALK ABOUT A FUZZY IDEA

(Summing it all up, one last time.)

What's the big deal?

What is it about homonaturality that people find the most objectionable? Is it the belief that it goes against the Bible? Is it the 'yucky-ness' of same-gender sex? Is it the belief that sex that doesn't create children is unnatural? Is it the fear that homonaturals want to lure and hurt their children? Is it too reflective of that me-first, inner part of all of us that we don't like to admit exists? Or is it the personal embarrassment we know we'll feel if we have to talk about it?

All of these objections to homonaturality are reasonable fears for people who want to maintain a faith and community where challenge to 'truth' is seen as threatening. While people may say that Truth is what they are holding onto, isn't it more often Tradition that is stronger? Tradition is always right there in front of us: ever-present; understandable, describable, predictable, and manageable. But Truth is always evolving: The world is flat; no, it's round. Gentiles are unclean; no, they're acceptable. Slavery is natural; no, it's immoral. Women are property; no, they're people with rights. Bare ankles are immoral; no, not even bare thighs are immoral.

Concerning Truth and Tradition

The trouble with Truth is that most of us rely on what someone else says is truth. And even if we do investigate it ourselves, we don't carry our investigation so far as to actually talk to the people we oppose. Instead we rely again on so-called evidence provided by people who tell us what we want to hear.

The trouble with Tradition is that most of us can't visualize what was 'traditionally' prevalent before our own lifetimes, and definitely not before the lifetimes of those who immediately preceded us. We like to think that what we believe is what everyone has believed for as long as the Bible has ever been quoted. But that is very clearly not the case if one really examines where Tradition has been and how it got here.

So what's really the problem?

Heteronaturality (attraction to opposite gender) has a side to it that the Bible opposes. It's called fornication and adultery. Most men who become pedophiles are heteronatural. There is probably just as great a percentage of heteronatural people who abuse others sexually as there are homonaturals who do the same. There is probably just as great a percentage of married heteronaturals who cheat on their spouses as there are homonaturals who look lustfully to another after having said "I will love and honor" to those special people in their lives. Heteronaturality (attraction to opposite gender) has a side to it that the Bible encourages. It's called Love and Marriage is one way of expressing that affection. But marriage is not demanded of every heteronatural person. It is desired, but not required. heteronatural people can be "in love", live together in complete physical commitment to one another and no one who knows them blinks an eye at what's going on. Even church-going folk can tolerate this living arrangement so long as they know the people and regard them as truly and monogamously devoted to one another. No one in this common-law situation is asked to resign from church membership. No one is prevented from participating in ministry or leadership.

The real problem is that most people cannot acknowledge that monogamous love and commitment is possible among homonatural persons. Various myths prevail among heteronatural people: (1) all or most homonaturals are unhappy; (2) all or most homonaturals are emotionally maladjusted; (3) all or most homonaturals are promiscuously-minded; (4) all or most homonaturals are incapable of Christian commitment; (5) all homonaturals are ineligible for God's grace and favor if they do not repent of their deviant lifestyle; and worst of all (6) homonaturals can be changed back into heteronaturals.

The only change that's really possible

If you were opposed to homonaturality before you started reading this article, you probably aren't going to change your mind based on just this small attempt to clarify things for you. If you were supportive of homonaturality, you probably aren't going to change your mind either.

We both have our standards of truth and we're confident that the other side has no interest in acknowledging ours. Is it a stalemate? Maybe, but not necessarily. I believe that God can do anything with anybody, but I don't believe He will go against the nature of the being he has created. Even if homonaturality was not in his mind at the beginning of time, I believe that it is now due to that feature of life from which diversity in all animals groups has evolved.

The number of species that exist today could not have existed at the time Noah was supposed to have preserved the chain of animal life. If they had, he would not have been able to account for them all. Even if you do not count the avian and aquatic species, there is still so many hundreds of thousands of land-locked species left that either Noah's story is a myth or evolution is responsible for the vast multiplication of species on this planet.

All life is in a state of change, not of quality, but of capability. Evolution dictates diversity and adaptability. With birth comes death. With age come degrees of diminishment. As wonder-full as progress is, it also brings toxicity, disease and exploitation. With opposite-gender sexuality comes variant sexuality. Not worse sexuality; not defective sexuality; just different sexuality.

Variance is natural, not diabolical. Variance is actually more desirable than uniformity. Uniformity would deny us seasons, discovery, and excellence. Tradition loves uniformity; it despises variance. Variance gives us more discomfort than any other influence.

Where do we go from here?

I believe the best thing to do is to 'plow like a farmer.' Fix your eye on a distant object and head toward it trying to keep your furrow as straight as possible. A good farmer doesn't choose an object in the same field he is plowing, but uses a reference point well beyond the field's edge because he still wants to have a somewhat distant guide when he reaches the end of the field.

I choose to have "perfect love" as the distant object in my life. It is a reference that is well beyond my own capability of reaching and is therefore more reliable that any reference I might find closer to where I live. The Bible is not my first choice. It is too close to me. At times it is like a guidepost at the edge of my field that allows me to digress more as I get closer to it. Every human being has written on his heart what the will of God is regarding faith, love and self-less-ness. We have the ability to project that image to any distance we want and then aim for it. The Bible has the limitation of culture-bound human involvement that distorts and obscures its real meaning in many areas. I know I run the risk of condemnation by the 'infallibility folk', but I don't see any more danger in challenging their theology than I do in ignoring love as the primary theme of God's will for my life.

The Bible should not be regarded as a clear and unmistakable product of inerrant creation, but as 'the most reliable information' people of old were given to find their way in a very confusing and frightening world. When we worship the Bible as an instrument of perfection, we surrender our responsibility to depend on the Holy Spirit for guidance. The miracle of revelation is not that God shows men's eyes what they must see, but that God helps men's minds understand what they don't see. Words help but they must not take the place of ideas. When they do, it is too easy to manipulate them in favor of our prejudices.

Ideas can never be reduced completely to printed words. Put another way, all words represent something bigger than themselves. Ideas require prayer, discussion, and discernment. It is for this very reason that printed words are not ideal: they entice mankind to absolve themselves of their duty to be attentive to what God wants to say to them right now, right here. Get out of the way and let the Holy Spirit do his work.

For the homonatural person who has not given herself over to the indulgent and perverse excesses normally ascribed to people of her orientation, printed words of Biblical condemnation are proving to be very traumatic when they are narrow-mindedly applied to the innocent as well as the guilty. When no allowance is made for the possible morality and faithfulness of homonatural people, the slander that is slammed in Romans 1:21 must be confessed by those traditionalists who erroneously live by the rule that "all are as guilty as some."

Who is F. P.?

We-Know-Who is a modern-day Pharisee who travels with his fundamentalist throng to protest at places where other groups are trying to create understanding about homosexuality. His method is an in-your-face bullhorn-and-placards assault with loud words and crude pictures that incite hate and violence. He says he is doing the work of the Lord, but his words and actions bear no resemblance to what you would expect from Jesus if he were here to show him how to act.

__Dear We-Know-Who__

Thank you for being the person you are. Your example is a good lesson for those among us who sometimes feel tempted to lower ourselves to the depths of depravity you pretend to oppose. Every time you appear somewhere protesting what you claim is against God's will, your very presence and actions do more to win for your opponents the hearts and minds of people who might have otherwise been fence-sitting. Until they see your embarrassing behavior, they may never take the time to declare how wrong you are. Keep it up. It helps us see the face of evil and helps us know what will become of us if we put more emphasis on judging than on loving.

ABOUT THE AUTHOR

As a line goes in one of my books, "I am a main-line denominational seminary drop-out" (40 years ago). That means I like to write and talk, mostly the former. My first lay ministry assignment was at a church for the deaf where I assisted a deaf pastor and deaf ongregation for 5½ years. I teach a sign language class to a half dozen residents who want to be able to converse with a new deaf resident that recently moved here.

We have a gay son and I have been active in trying to help people understand that there is more than one sexual orientation. We also have two daughters who married fundamentalist husbands. Although the girls love their brother, they do not want him to discuss his "lifestyle" with them or their children. My goal in all my writing is to someday influence them to be more understanding and tolerant.

It seems as if people who are like-minded about homonaturality have been placed in our path in all the places where we have lived from Hawaii to New Jersey and from Michigan to Texas. Some were gay and some were straight. We thank God everyday that He has allowed us to encounter such helpful and supportive friends during our 53 years of marriage. God is still speaking and we are still listening.